Hercules

You there! Think you're strong, do you? Think you're a fighter? Suppose a lion came strolling by. Suppose a python came sliding along. What good would your fists be to you then?

There's not a soul who can crush a stone in his fist or uproot a hollybush barehanded. There's not a man born but a rabbit can outrun him, a ferret outfight him, a cockroach endure more hardships. Not one. Not now.

Listen! before the constellations of beasty stars are herded away into the far distant barns of night. Once there was such a man. Once there was Hercules.

As strong as the moon that drags the sea up the land, as strong as the glacier that carves out a valley, as strong as the sun that cracks open the dry earth, that was Hercules. Listen! before the god who holds up the sky grows weary and lets it fall—because there is no one now who could prevent it crashing on to the place beneath.

Hercules is gone.

Geraldine McCaughrean has written over a hundred books for children and adults. After many years spent working for a London publisher, she now writes full-time. Her novels have won her the Whitbread, Carnegie, *Guardian*, UKRA, Smarties, and Beefeater Awards. She has also written plays for stage and radio. Among her other books for Oxford University Press are *A Little Lower than the Angels*, *A Pack of Lies*, *Plundering Paradise*, *The Kite Rider*, and *Stop the Train*.

Hercules

Other books by Geraldine McCaughrean

Hercules

Geraldine McCaughrean

OXFORD
UNIVERSITY PRESS

OXFORD
UNIVERSITY PRESS

Great Clarendon Street, Oxford OX2 6DP

Oxford University Press is a department of the University of Oxford.
It furthers the University's objective of excellence in research, scholarship,
and education by publishing worldwide in

Oxford New York

Auckland Cape Town Dar es Salaam Hong Kong Karachi
Kuala Lumpur Madrid Melbourne Mexico City Nairobi
New Delhi Shanghai Taipei Toronto

With offices in

Argentina Austria Brazil Chile Czech Republic France Greece
Guatemala Hungary Italy Japan Poland Portugal Singapore
South Korea Switzerland Thailand Turkey Ukraine Vietnam

Oxford is a registered trade mark of Oxford University Press
in the UK and in certain other countries

British Library Cataloguing in Publication Data available

ISBN-13: 978-0-19-274200-1
ISBN-10: 0-19-274200-0

3 5 7 9 10 8 6 4

Typeset by AFS Image Setters Ltd, Glasgow

Printed and bound in Great Britain by
Cox & Wyman Ltd, Reading, Berkshire

1

The Son of Zeus

The first time Zeus created Humankind, he used gold. Of course he did. Zeus had every precious substance at his fingertips, and an eye for beauty. Unfortunately the Race of Gold had an eye for beauty, too, for no sooner were they moulded and cast and buffed up to a shine than they began to prance and preen, and pride themselves on their looks.

'How beautiful we are! How fine! How precious! Who will treasure us? Who will admire us? Who will worship us and do our bidding?'

Zeus melted them down and ground their golden bones into dust which he sprinkled into the rivers.

The second time, he used silver. It had a ghostly loveliness and was agreeably soft within his clever hands.

The Race of Silver was elegant and effete. They did not prance about or flaunt their sinuous silvery beauty. In fact they scarcely moved at all. When they were not thinking beautiful thoughts, they were gazing at spiders' webs sprinkled with dew or stroking the silky strands of each other's hair or watching their breath cloud their own shining kneecaps. When they lay down and slept, they rarely woke up again.

Zeus piled hills on their sleeping forms and turned instead to bronze. The Race of Bronze was bursting with energy and needed little sleep. It was tireless and hard-working and brutally strong. It tore down spiders' webs in gathering wood for its forges, and on these forges it made spades and mattocks and hoes, armour and knives and spears. Once the Race of Bronze discovered war, they were happy indeed. The fields lay fallow and the beds unslept in . . . for the Men of Bronze were busily slaughtering one another with mace and arrow and sword.

Zeus had no need to destroy them. They killed each other, leaving their brazen bones scattered about among the ruins of their fallen forts.

There was nothing left but iron. Iron and earth and clay. Rather than dirty his hands, Zeus gave the work over to Prometheus the Titan. Once, before their conquest by the Olympians, the Titans had ruled Heaven and Earth. Now Zeus could snap his fingers and the few surviving Titans were obliged to do his dirty work.

But it was a good choice. Prometheus was a master craftsman. Despite being given such poor quality materials, his big hands twisted the iron into a delicate filigree of bone, and clad it in coarse clay with a topknot of grass. He lavished the tenderest care on his little manikins and grew fond of them, for all their imperfections.

When they asked *Who? When? Where?* and *What?* Prometheus taught them the Sciences. When they gazed up at him, in their innocence, and asked *Why?* he taught them the Arts—Music, Painting, Poetry, and Dance. When they shivered in their furless, goosy skin, he even climbed to the mountaintops and plucked a glimmer of Fire from the wheel of the Sun Chariot to warm Mankind.

2

Zeus was enraged. 'Steal fire from the gods? Give fire into the hands of those . . . those . . . *termites*? I'll make you pay, Titan! I'll make you wish you were never born. I'll make you wish you had become extinct like the rest of your kind!' And he took Prometheus and chained him, spread-eagled, against the Caucasus Mountains, a prisoner for all time. Eagles tore at his unprotected stomach, from dawn to dusk, feeding on his liver, rending at his liver, shredding it with their beaks. But because Prometheus was immortal and because the liver can heal and renew itself, there was no end to his Titanic pain. There was no end to Zeus's revenge. There was no end to the guilty knowledge in every Human heart: '*We* did that to Prometheus. He stole fire for *us*. He is suffering for *us*.'

Why do I tell you this? I don't know. It all happened thousands of years before Hercules was born.

And yet the picture would not be complete without that background skyline, without those distant crags specked red by Prometheus's torment. It tells you something about the gods. It tells you something about strength and weakness, about tyranny and freedom.

'Strangle him. Bite on him. *Crush him in your coils!*' raged the queen of the gods, thrusting her face so low that her cheeks flushed with blood.

The two serpents coiled around the base of her throne were as thick as jungle creepers and sleeved in overlapping scales as large and green as leaves. They blinked their hooded eyes, and their forked tongues flickered lovingly around her cheeks and ears. 'We hear, O Hera. Yes-s-s, Hercules-s-s sh-shall die.'

'Another woman's child,' she seethed.

'We hear, O Hera.'

'Fathered by my husband!'

3

'He dies-s-s, O Queen.'

' . . . made me the laughing stock of all heaven!'

'S-s-surely not, O Queen.'

'Imagine! The king of heaven preferring a common mortal woman to me, his sloe-eyed queen!'

'S-s-sloe-eyed, but not slow to see,' whispered the grovelling serpents in her ear. 'We go, O Queen, to s-s-strangle the puny child in his cradle, to s-s-smother him as he s-s-sleeps-s-s.' And they slithered across the marble floor of heaven like two streams of fetid green water, trickling over the brink of the clouds.

The baby's cradle stood in the shade of the eaves, and his hands reached for the lazy flies that circled overhead. His mother Alcmene was indoors sleeping through the heat of the day. So too was the king she had married after Hercules was born. Not a grand king, nor one who lived in a grand palace, but one who had come to love his little stepson. His gardens were greenly watered, and the air was filled with the scent of azaleas, and with silence.

So at the sound of a scurrying rattle, the baby smiled and looked around. Two heaving heaps of green, quivering and shivering, fumed like compost heaps on either side of the cradle. Out of the thorny heaps, horny heads rose up, wavering; gaping wide red mouths with flickering tongues and bared, pronging fangs. Venom dripped on the bedclothes and scorched large, sizzling holes.

'*Strangle him. Bite on him. Crush him in your coils,*' murmured the leaves on the trees. The baby boy laughed out loud at the ducking dance of the serpents' swaying heads. He reached out and took each by its thick green throat.

Their hinged jaws gaped. Their tails slumped, coil upon coil, into the crib on top of the baby's legs. Their thrashing rocked the wooden bed so that its feet thumped on the wooden verandah. The noise woke Queen Alcmene in her room overhead, and looking out of her window, she clutched at her hair: 'My child! My Hercules! Save my Hercules! O Zeus in heaven, our baby!'

The young child looked up at her and smiled at the sight of his mother's face. And he held up the snakes— one in each hand—as if to say, 'Look what I've got!' He jabbed his nose into their red mouths, saying, 'Aboo! Aboo!' Venom trickled down their scaly trunks.

First he knotted their necks. Then he knotted their tails. He plucked off their scales like petals off a daisy, and he bit into their soft, sheeny bellies to see what was inside.

'Dead! Dead! My darlings!' murmured the wind in the hollow trees of the garden.

At last Hercules dropped the serpents out of the crib and watched rather sadly as their lifeless coils slumped one by one out on to the floor. Then his mother came running along the verandah outstretched like a bird, her clothes billowing. He turned on her a pair of doleful eyes, then looked over the side of his cot at one of the snakes and said, with a trembling chin, 'Broke it.'

For all Hercules was not his own son, King Amphitryon took a burning pride in the boy as he grew. No expense or trouble was too great when it came to his education. One tutor was not enough: the king's stepson must have three—one to teach him wisdom, one to teach him sport, and one to teach him music. Eminent men they were, all three. But neither Rhadamanthus (with his wise sayings) nor Linus (with his lutes) could fire Hercules with a desire to learn. Only his sports-master, Chiron, could do that. Perhaps the fact that Chiron was a centaur—half man and half horse—made the difference. From discus-throwing to steeplechasing, there was no sport at which Chiron did not excel, and Hercules longed to be like him. Because Chiron told him to, he found it no hardship to get up early, go to bed early, and run and exercise for long hours every day.

One day the centaur said, 'Never touch strong drink, lad.'

'When do I ever get offered strong drink,' said the eleven-year-old Hercules laughing.

But Chiron stamped his hind hooves and said with uncharacteristic fierceness, 'Promise me!' Hercules promised without a second thought.

Not that Hercules was slow at his other subjects. In fact he played a lute rather well, though his fingers had a tendency to snap the strings. And he soon knew every one of Rhadamanthus's wise and pompous sayings, and would teeter and stoop along the corridors wagging his finger and, in a piping voice, doing his Rhadamanthus impersonation: 'The heart is bigger than the fist.' 'A bad man may be punished by the gods but only a good one is envied by them.' 'Folly is the fool's choice.' 'Hardship is the hero's pride.' Whether he understood them, that was a different matter. He learned the words . . . and he did do a splendid impression of Rhadamanthus. It was a pity there were so few people to appreciate it. When his mother saw it, she only told him not to be disrespectful.

In those days, Thebes was a small place, keeping itself to itself. It was uncommon to see strangers in the area unless they were passing by on the road. So Hercules looked once and looked again when he saw two women in a tree one day.

He had been stalking a deer through the woods, and his eyes ached from searching out its blotched hide among the dapple of the trees. He lost sight of it for a moment, and when he once more discerned a moving shape among the blobby sunlight, it was not the deer at all but a woman dressed in austere grey. She went and stood in the hollow of a tree—as if it were a doorway— and Hercules's eye was drawn up the trunk to where another blousy-looking woman in dark red and black slouched along a branch, like a kill draped there by a lion. 'Greetings, Hercules,' said the second woman in a liquid, mellifluous voice. 'Come nearer. There's so much I could give you . . .'

Hercules was rather embarrassed: the other woman, upright in the alcove of the tree, made him feel uncomfortable, watching him with her uneven, grey eyes. Even the birds were not singing: they had been thrown off-key by a skirl of unearthly music blowing through the wood. 'Yes, come nearer, Hercules. Show us what manner of man you are.'

Man! Ha! He was only thirteen! So to overcome his awkwardness and a feeling that someone was about to make a terrible mistake, he moved towards the tree doing his funny 'Rhadamanthus' walk, tottering and hinnying and wagging one finger in the air.

As he reached a spot beneath the branches, the woman in red rolled startlingly off her perch and dropped down behind him. Her feet made hardly a sound. Her arm circled his shoulders and her mouth pressed against his ear: 'I know what *you'll* choose.'

In some panic, Hercules looked to the other woman but she had folded her arms across her chest and remained inside the hollow tree. Her face was quite blank: she simply said, 'Well? Which *do* you choose? Hardship or happiness? Danger or daydreams? To struggle and to suffer, or to sleep?'

Hercules giggled maniacally. 'I think you've got the wrong . . .'

'You are Hercules the Strong, aren't you? Son of Alcmene?' snapped the grey woman.

The other, in red and black, ran her fingers over the muscles of Hercules's arm. 'Oooh, yes. He's strong all right.'

'And slow-witted seemingly. Well? Choose, boy. You're privileged, you know. Most don't get the choice. Hardship or ease? We haven't got all day: other people have fates to be decided.'

Afterwards, people asked him, 'What possessed you? What came over you? Who in their right mind . . . ?' But at the time it wasn't like that. Hercules simply felt awkward, and the words they were using brought to mind all Rhadamanthus's pompous, ponderous sayings. So he put on his Rhadamanthus stoop, and did his comical Rhadamanthus walk, and recited two or three epigrams in the scholar's thin, piping voice. Anything to break the tension.

' "Hardship is the hero's pride." "Fame was never found in bed." ' (He wagged his finger: it was a very good impersonation.) ' "Failure is easy, success is hard!" '

The grey woman's eyes, at first dismayed by the faces he was pulling, suddenly flashed. 'True! That's perfectly true!'

The red woman's hand slipped off his stooping shoulders. 'You mean you choose hardship and danger? *Nobody* does that. Nobody *ever* does that. Everybody chooses an easy life!'

' "Danger is the pathway from cowardice to Fame!" ' hinnied Hercules, too busy racking his brains for more sayings to pay much attention. ' "Folly is the fool's choice!" '

'Pompous little brat,' said the woman in red, and turning to the other she said, 'So you've won one at last, Virtue. Good riddance, I say.'

The woman in grey seemed equally surprised. Her

8

sharp, precise voice bobbed with delight. 'How very heartening. Still, you can't say I wasn't due for a win. Nobody has chosen a life of hardship and suffering for two hundred years now. Come along, Vice. Fasten your fastenings—and do at least braid your hair: you look a real slummock. Don't dawdle now.'

Together they strode away through the trees, Virtue and Vice. Hercules called after them: 'Hey! Where are you going? Anyway—who are you?'

The women linked arms and looked back at him quizzically. 'Don't worry,' said the woman in grey cheerfully. 'Your wish is granted. You shall live a life of struggle and suffering. Fame, danger, pain, work—all of those. I'll see to it. Extraordinary . . . ' (She turned back to her companion.) 'I really expected this one to choose you, Vice.'

And Hercules was left standing on one foot, his finger still pointing foolishly at the sky, his face gradually losing any likeness to old Rhadamanthus. Even the strange, haunting music faded away, and the birds rediscovered their voices. Hercules tried to remember the tune . . .

Inside the house, Linus, the music teacher, was crouched over his lute. A vague, short-sighted young man, he had difficulty remembering what time of day it was. When Hercules arrived for a lesson, Linus always supposed it must be time to give one. So when Hercules ran into the room humming loudly, and sat down at once, and took a lute on his lap, and picked at it, Linus stood up.

'Good morning, Hercules.'

'Shsshsh!'

'Don't shsshsh me, boy!'

'Shsshsh! I'm trying to remember a tune.' (He tried

9

to pick out the mysterious music on his lute, but could not find the right key.)

'It might help if you held the lute properly,' said Linus.

'Be quiet, can't you? I'm forgetting it! Mmmm . . . hmmmm . . . hmmmm . . . '

'*Wrist*, boy. How often do I have to tell you—keep that wrist arched.'

'Oh please! Quiet! Mmmmm . . . hmmmmm . . . hmmmm . . . ' But the haunting tune was dribbling out of his head like sand out of a fist.

'That fourth string is flat. Haven't I taught you yet? You can't ever play a lute till you've tuned it. Let me have it.' And Linus tried to take the lute out of Hercules's lap.

'Give it here!' protested Hercules. But already the tune had soaked away like spilled water and was lost everlastingly.

So unnerved was Hercules by his meeting with the two women, so lost was the piece of music, that Hercules's frayed temper snapped. Linus had hold of the body of the lute; Hercules had hold of the neck. With a turn of the wrist he wrenched the instrument away from his teacher and swung it like a club. His eyes were shut with fury.

He heard the lute crush like an egg-shell. He felt the broken strings coil back around his wrists and hands. When he opened his eyes, he thought that Linus must have run from the room in fright: he waited for the man's pale, refined face to reappear at the open door. Then he saw, at the other end of the slippery marble floor a heap of familiar clothes.

Hercules retreated to the other end of the room and sat down in a corner. Strangely enough, he could remember the ragged tune perfectly now. He was still humming it when the king came into the room. 'What are you doing there, boy? Aren't you supposed to be with Chiron doing sports? Where's Linus? I need a lutenist tomorrow at dinner. There are visitors. Important visitors . . . Hercules? Boy? Answer me.'

Hercules looked up and showed the stump of his lute still festooned with curling, broken cat-gut. 'Why am I so strong, father? Why? Other boys aren't so . . . I killed him, father. I didn't mean to. But I killed Linus.'

2

Broken Promises

They told Hercules that Linus was not dead at all—only stunned—and that when he came round, he was so angry that he had taken ship for Syria.

Hercules would have liked to believe them.

They told him that no boy of thirteen could kill a man with one blow of a lute. He wanted to believe them. He wanted so much to believe them that, by the following night, he almost did.

Only when the important visitors arrived (King Eurytus of Oechalia and his daughter, Iole), and the king asked Hercules to play his lute, did the boy hold the instrument on his knees and weep.

Princess Iole came and stood in front of him. 'What's the matter?' she asked in a whisper, purposely placing herself between Hercules and the adults so that they would not see him crying.

'Nothing . . . someone died. Someone I knew.'

'I'm very sorry. I hope they had a good life first.'

Hercules looked up. Princess Iole was about twelve, with sand-coloured hair scorched gold on the crown by being out in the sun. 'Which do you think is best? To live a life of comfort and wealth or struggle and heroism?' he said.

'Who for? Best for whom?' said Iole, screwing up her eyes. 'Comfort and wealth are best if you've got children or elderly relations,' (and she waved a hand in the direction of her father), 'but personally I'd prefer a little adventure, even if it meant sleeping in cactus bushes and eating worms.' Hercules's jaw dropped.

Hurriedly he wiped his face with his sleeve. 'Whatever must you think of me?'

She did not even pause for reflection. 'I think you have lovely hands, but you're an odd shape. Look at you—you're as wide from side to side as you are from head to foot: you're square.'

Hercules stood up and looked down at himself. 'You mean I'm fat?'

'No. Just square. And you don't look a bit like your father or your sister.'

'That's because he's not my father. He's my stepfather. And Megara is my stepsister.'

'Is she more important than you? Is she older?'

'She'll be queen of Thebes one day. I won't because I'm not the king's true son.'

'Was your real father square, too? Who was he?'

'I don't know. I don't know who he was.' Her questions swooped at him until he felt like a berry tree stripped bare by the birds. But Hercules was not offended. Nobody had ever shown such an interest in him before.

Iole was not square. She was long and rounded, rather like a lute. He wanted to pick her up and find out what music came out of her. She did not take after her father, either. King Eurytus was long and thin with nobbles here and there, like bamboo. He giggled a great deal: the more wine he drank, the more he giggled. Seeing Iole and

Hercules still talking an hour later, he giggled uncontrollably. 'Looks like an alliance is forming between Thebes and Oechalia,' he snorted, pointing rudely. 'Why not? How about it, Amphitryon? Your stepson and my daughter. Let's make a royal match of it.'

'Aren't they a little young for such things,' said Amphitryon quietly, seeing Hercules blush.

'When they're older, then! My word on it! If he wants her, he shall have her!'

Later that night, Hercules still sat plucking his lute in the deserted banqueting room. His mother, passing the doorway, saw him and came closer. 'I hope you've put that other matter right out of your head,' she said, stroking his hair.

Hercules had. His mind was full of Iole. He said, 'Can I marry her? I want to marry her. She's lovely.'

It was his mother's turn to laugh. 'Gracious! Such thoughts at your age! Your first love, eh? That's nice, dear . . . But King Eurytus had had rather a lot to drink. I doubt if he'll remember what he said, tomorrow.' And away she went, content because Hercules was not moping about the death of his music teacher. She did not hear Hercules say softly, 'But *I* will. *I'll* remember.'

As Hercules grew, there was no concealing his phenomenal strength. There was no denying the likeness to his father, the king of heaven, whose arms, since the start of time, could strangle every snaking river, buckle the interfolded hills, and shoulder the sands of time into dunes of history. Not that Hercules knew who his father was. In fact he found it rather embarrassing that clothes stretched round his square frame looked like washing draped on a mountainside to dry, and that the lute strings broke beneath his fingers like thread. He said goodbye to old

Rhadamanthus, and Chiron his sports-master left Thebes as well. While he grew, he nursed the secret certainty that he would one day marry Iole. Then they would leave Thebes and travel the world in search of adventure, sleeping in cactus bushes and (if need be) eating worms. After all, his present life promised no hardship or suffering.

As Hercules grew, Thebes seemed to shrink. Once, its stone city walls had been his furthest horizon; now he could judge it for the small, vulnerable muddle of houses it was, with its belt of low stonewalling and few prosperous farms. When the young men of neighbouring Menia had been drinking, they galloped across the plain, across the carefully tended fields, and threw lighted brands over the wall. An alarm of clanking fire buckets woke the town and set the women screaming.

What began as drunken vandalism grew into a sport. The young men of Menia would dare one another to greater and greater mischief. Young Theban women were kidnapped. Theban wagons outside the city were stoned and looted. Dirty slogans were daubed on the city wall. The crops in the fields were put to the torch. Never a night went by without some wanton act of destruction, some flurry within the town. The citizens protested daily to the king.

Amphitryon protested to the king of Menia, but got the impression that he was rather proud of his wild young men. The next night nobody said so, but everyone knew, that the boys of Menia were coming in force for a pitched battle. Thebes closed its gates.

When they came, they were carrying shields and long staves which they banged against the shields with a taunting rhythm. They speared the ground with firebrands, and the grassy area in front of the gates was as light as day. Then they brought out a battering ram. The boys of Menia meant to take the town.

A new kind of panic gripped the city. Its army was small. It was too late to send for help. Hercules, watching from the high windows of the royal house, could see the commotion in the streets and hear the cries of panic.

Walking slowly down to the gate-yard, he watched the bending and splintering of the big wooden doors. Soon they would buckle inwards in front of the Menian battering ram. Sorry to see damage to a perfectly fine pair of gates, he opened the small, pedestrian side-door to the left of the barred gates. Looking over his shoulder at the mustered army of Thebes, he said, 'Well? Are you coming?'

Have you ever stood up to your knees in a cold sea, wishing you had the courage to go deeper, and had some stalwart soul wade past you, thigh-, waist-, chest-, neck-deep with not so much as a gasp at the cold? That was the kind of envious admiration the men of Thebes felt as seventeen-year-old Hercules waded in among the Menian rabble, one-deep, five-deep, fifteen-deep and was quite lost from sight. Only his fists now and then showed above the mob. Pricked with shame, Amphitryon's few soldiers went after him.

Have you ever watched an ebb tide strand the sea on a beach and shred the water into larger and larger holes? That was how the attacking mob from Menia fell to pieces at the hands of Theban Hercules. With one man lifted up and flung over-arm, he flattened a row of ten more. With one shield snatched from the hands of a lout, he sliced through a row of shields. When he heard the ominous scrape of swords being drawn from their scabbards, and saw an archer taking aim from the platform of a chariot, he put his shoulder to the chariot and left the archer sprawled beneath it like a turtle under its shell, the horse scattering the swordsmen.

They fell back. They called on the gods for protection

from 'this bull', 'this tyrant', 'this barbarian!' They ran, full of such terror that they outran the Theban men and left them to hurl stones and laugh abuse after them. Hercules simply turned away and walked back into the city, deep in thought. It surprised him when his stepfather, sweating and panting and sword drawn, fell on his neck and kissed him. 'You were magnificent, son! Magnificent! You left nothing for us to do! You swatted them like a swarm of flies!'

'They were so puny,' said Hercules with an embarrassed shrug.

'You struck terror into them, that's why!' Amphitryon was dancing round him, almost drunk with delight and pride. 'There's only one reward befitting a show of manhood like that. There's only one way I can show you how *grateful* I am . . . She's yours. Megara is yours. I give her to you—and with her the right to wear the crown of Thebes when I'm gone!' He looked for Hercules's face to light up, and saw it drop instead.

'But what about Iole?'

'Where? What's Iole?'

'Princess Iole. Of Oechalia. I can't marry them both!'

Amphitryon saw his daughter coming. He was anxious to tell her the good news. 'Zeus! I had no idea you remembered that plain little thing. Don't trouble yourself. She's already married, just this last month. Eurytus married her to some potentate. No, your way is open to take Megara—and may you live out your days in contentment and prosperity here in Thebes!'

Megara caught these last words of her father's and looked her stepbrother up and down with startled alarm. 'Me? Marry Hercules? But he's . . . he's . . . ' and her eyes rifled him up and down in search of a suitable adjective.

'Square,' said Hercules feelingly, and offered his stepsister his arm.

As any sister would, she slapped it.

They were not unhappy. They liked each other . . . as brother and sister can. Their family grew—a new baby every year, another room filled with crying in the royal house—and Thebes shrank still further in Hercules's eyes. Sometimes it felt like a chain round his chest that stopped him taking a deep breath.

Still, Megara was a decent girl even if she was not Iole. And his children were a wonder to Hercules. He would play with them for hours, and watch their fists rend feebly at their toys, and love them for their fragile helplessness. Whenever he walked about the grounds, festooned in clinging babies and toddlers, he knew that the two peculiar women in the forest were utter liars: this was not a life of hardship and suffering.

It was simply a matter of making time one day to kill King Eurytus for breaking his promise.

One day King Amphitryon was bitten by a snake. Not a large snake or a deadly one. He drank some wine to dull the pain, and by dinner time showed no ill effects but for a little tetchiness. At dinner, he raised a toast: 'To Thebes—may we all live and die here!' He noticed, with some vexation, that Hercules did not drink the toast.

'You know I don't drink, father,' said Hercules. 'I promised Chiron I would never . . . '

'Not drink a toast to Thebes? Just because you weren't born here!'

Hercules said, 'It's not that at all. I'll drink it in water if you like. Chiron told me . . . '

'Drink a toast in water? You may as well not drink it at all. It's an insult, an affront.'

'Just a little wine,' whispered his mother to Hercules, 'for the sake of good manners.'

'Manners before principles?' Hercules whispered back.

'Don't be pompous,' whispered Megara on the other side of him. 'Look how you've upset father.'

'Why father won't drink wine?' lisped the oldest child loudly.

'Because he's obstinate,' said the queen.

'Because he hates Thebes,' said Amphitryon angrily chafing his bitten leg.

'Because some old nag told him not to,' said Megara waspishly.

Hercules's temper snapped. 'Very well, I'll drink! I'll drink if you insist! To Thebes! May I live and die here in soggy prosperity!' and he emptied his cup. 'What if I did give my word to Chiron? Who keeps promises? Even kings don't keep promises. Take King Eurytus . . . ' He reached across and drank Amphitryon's wine as well. 'Though why a man should want to live and die in one place I don't know. How is the world better off for that? And why a man should marry his own sister for the sake of it . . . ' He spilled some of Megara's wine in snatching it out of her hand to drink. It made a large red stain over her heart.

The wine tasted good. It warmed him. He thought that if he drank enough, it might dissolve the hard, painful knot of anger in his stomach. But instead of dissolving, the anger swelled.

The little snake that had bitten the king still lay curled in a corner. But for the noise that followed, you might have heard it whisper, *'How long you made me wait, Hercules, for your destruction. But now I have you. Now!'*

Hera, queen of the gods, did not wait to see the result of her plotting but slithered out through a crevice into darkening night.

3

Hera's Doom

Hercules drank every cup of wine laid out along the table and demanded more from the servants. The walls began to heave and melt, the floor to lurch under his feet so that he fell against the table. The table dared to bruise him, so he picked it up and tore off its legs one by one. The doors of the room seemed to gape foolishly, like dumb mouths. He hurled chairs and stools into the stupid holes, and gagged the laughing windows with rugs torn up from the floor. It felt as though he was running through a long tunnel filled with cobwebs that caught round his head and made his eyes dimmer and dimmer, his ears deafer and deafer, his mouth full of sticky threads: he had to drink more wine to be rid of the taste.

Unable to focus, he was maddened by shrill little voices all around him: like whining mosquitos, they maddened him. He struck out to be rid of them, and kicked out at the soft, clinging demons that seemed to be dragging at his knees, trying to trip him up.

Who was that sitting in Amphitryon's chair, shrieking 'Stop! Stop! Stop!'? Eurytus? When had Eurytus been asked to the dinner?

'You know what I'm going to do to you, you shyster?' said Hercules, though his mouth seemed to be full of stones. 'I'm going to push your promises down your lying throat. Die, you lying scum!' And he trampled over unseen barricades of soft, hard, and unidentifiable objects, his feet and fists crushing everything that came between him and his revenge.

Perfidious Eurytus—he ducked away at the last moment, and let Hercules crash headfirst into the wall. A bloody blackness trickled down out of his hairline and swamped his brain in darkness. Hercules fell in a heap amidst the rubble of his own making.

When he came to, he was still lying there, and Amphitryon—it wasn't Eurytus at all—was still in his seat, though his head was bowed down as far as his knees. Dead on the floor lay two servants, Queen Alcmene, Megara, and, huddled round her like little broken boats smashed by a storm, all his six small children.

At the sound of Hercules's cry, Amphitryon started up in his chair and snatched up a copper ladle to defend himself. But when he saw Hercules's face, he laid it down again.

'What happened? Who did this?' said Hercules, on his hands and knees.

'Who did it? *Who did it?* You did it, Hercules. You kicked and pounded everything and everyone here into the Realm of Shadows. You trampled on your daughters, you pulled up your sons like weeds and threw them away. You murdered my wife and you murdered the wife I gave you out of my own flesh and blood. When the servants tried to restrain you, you broke their necks. Only the gods reaching out of heaven put a stop to your massacre. They hurled you against that wall—and I wish they had thrown you all the way to the Underworld.

21

You're not human, you. You've got more strength than a man and less pity than a beast . . . And I'm as bad as you. Because I made you drink.'

'Chiron told me . . . '

'I know what Chiron told you. But something drove me to make you break your word to him. Now I'm punished for it. Now I must keep the promise I made to your mother the day I married her. I swore always to protect you, life and limb. Protect you? Ha! What executioner could lay hands on you anyway? Protect *you*!'

Hercules stared at his two hands as though they were trusted friends who had unaccountably betrayed him. 'I *want* to die. I want it. Send an executioner now! My guilt is crushing me like rocks and boulders! If you won't punish me, I call on the gods to condemn me!'

A beam of light, as thickly bright as a column of solid brass, broke through the deep windows of the room. It bleached the floor where it touched, and a solar wind howled around the room.

From the slopes of Olympus, the king of the gods stared at the royal house of Thebes until, like a snail beneath a burning glass, it started to writhe. The lesser gods and goddesses stood silent, at a distance, half-turned away out of embarrassment. Fancy the king of the gods showing such distress over the fate of a mere mortal man. Justice surely demanded that Hercules should die. How long would Zeus hesitate before he struck the young murderer down?

A convulsive shiver shook his huge, blue-robed frame, then Zeus sat bolt upright on his throne. 'Can he help it if he has my strength in his arms? Or my fire in his core? It's a burden too great for any poor boy! Only a god could bear it . . . The drink was responsible, not Hercules!

Amphitryon was responsible, for making him drink! Hercules shan't die! My son shan't die!'

The gods murmured among themselves and shot nervous glances at Hera, knowing that the queen of the gods loathed and detested Hercules. But to their surprise, Hera showed no irritation when Hercules was spared. Toying affectionately with the faithful little snake in her lap she listened then coughed politely. 'You are right, of course, my love. What purpose will it serve to strike Hercules dead? Or to lock him away in prison? Bind him in service instead, to . . . to whom? I know! Bind him in slavery to his cousin, the king of Argos. Slavery will save Hercules from the sin of pride, and the world will see that he has been punished for killing those few paltry people.'

Zeus cast on his wife a look of grateful love such as she had not seen for many earthly generations. She blushed, and the little snake squirmed away among her clothing. 'That's a fine idea, Hera! That *shall* be Hercules's sentence! See where I carve it in fire on the walls of Thebes: *Hercules is bound in slavery to the king of Argos, that the gods may be praised. Let him serve and obey!*'

And the lesser gods and goddesses saw Hera roll her head on her beautiful, snake-like neck and smile as the cobra smiles. 'Die long and die hard, Hercules,' she whispered, 'at the hands of that *little* man. Let it never be written that the finger of Zeus struck you a glorious blow, nor that you died young and painlessly. *Suffer*, bastard. *Suffer*, you child of damned Alcmene! SUFFER!'

When Hercules read his doom written by fire on the walls of Thebes, he left at once for Argos. He took with him nothing but the clothes he wore, and would gladly have left those behind, because they were stained with his children's blood.

King Eurystheus of Argos was in every way a *little* man. His little head lolled between narrow shoulders and his small eyes kept secret his little thoughts. He prided himself quietly on the slenderness of his wrists from which his small hands drooped like unripe fruit. The walls of his palace were so thick, and the rooms inside so cluttered with ornaments, that he picked his way through narrow canyons of furniture and was overshadowed with lamps. When beggars begged at his gates, they got little charity. And when the people of his realm pleaded for his protection from the dark forces of the great World Beyond, they got small comfort. His heart had shrunk for want of love inside it, and he belittled the achievements of everyone but himself.

The only things about Eurystheus that were not small and mean were his coffers of treasure, his cowardice, and his vicious, inventive cruelty. He prayed to the goddess Hera for relief from his boredom . . . and she sent him Prince Hercules as a bond-slave. 'Excellent goddess!' He was only sorry that his new toy would so soon be worn out and broken. 'Have that criminal crawl to my throne on his knees!' he crowed. Hercules obeyed.

'So! Slave! What can I find for a drunken child-murderer to do in my spotless realm? Your hands are too bloody for you to stay inside *my* palace.'

Hercules crouched on one knee, his head bowed.

'Not so big as I expected,' said Eurystheus. 'I thought they said you were a strong man. You're quite squat really.'

'Square,' said Hercules.

'Don't you dare to open your mouth in my presence, *serf*!' piped Eurystheus, startled by the size of Hercules's voice. 'This morning I did you the honour of thinking about you briefly. And I have thought of a fitting task for a butcher like you. The people of Nemea—one of the least significant towns in my realm—keep whining to me about some little lion. Apparently it's taken to killing children . . . A relation of yours, perhaps, ha ha ha! Kill it. What are you waiting for? That's all. Kill it.'

Hercules stood up and moved towards the door.

'Ah, but cousin!' called Eurystheus. 'Don't trouble to burden yourself with a sword or spear or bow or anything, will you? I hear the creature's hide is too thick to cut. It's killed two hundred hunters already.'

Hercules nodded without turning back to face the king, and strode out of the palace.

'He'll run away,' said Eurystheus with a snort of disdain. 'The goddess Hera didn't think of that. He'll run and hide himself. That squat oaf won't be back.'

The lion of Nemea turned over his latest kill with a large velvety paw. He did not do as other lions do, and haul his dead meat up into the safety of a tree. For the scavenger had not been born that dared to rob the Nemean Lion.

A new scent tingled in his velvet nostrils—a smell of warm meat salty with sweat: a salt that longed to be licked, a meat that asked to be eaten, a smell that begged to be tasted. He stood on top of his kill, and looked about.

The square, two-legged creature that he saw did not stir the lion's slow-pumping heart. A small meal. But the strange way it was standing excited his curiosity. It was leaning on a massive club of wood, one foot crossed casually over the other, and its eyes fixed on him. It looks at me, but it surely cannot see me, or it would tremble, thought the lion, and went closer, closer, and closer still. In fact he prowled tight round the legs of the two-legged creature, curling his tail around its shins and snuffing up the peculiar smell. Always before, these man-beasts had smelt of acrid, delicious fear. This prey only smelt of porridge and soap and milk and the sweat of a long journey.

'*Raaow!*' said the lion, and his cavernous mouth opened as wide as the stocky shoulders of his prey. But the shoulders did not flinch. Instead, the creature set whirling the club in its fist, making mesmerizing circles in front of the lion's eyes, and brought the club down with titanic force on the lion's velvety skull.

The Nemean Lion was thrown half a league by the blow . . . but landed on all four paws and came back at a run—a level-leaping run that ate up the ground. It launched itself at Hercules's head, all teeth and gullet and reaching claws.

Hercules ducked.

The lion writhed in the air and landed, rampant, in a bed of cactus. Once again it rushed at Hercules and, opening its jaws, received the unexpected meal of a club of wood rammed into its throat. It chewed and spat and swallowed.

Fed with meat and wood, dazed with clubbing, and burning with cactus needles, the Nemean Lion turned for its cave, thinking to gather its strength. But as it ran, Hercules ran after it, right to the mouth of the cave, and beyond. He braved the stench, he braved the bones, he braved the sudden dark. The lion shrank to a glimmering pair of green eyes; its noise swelled to an earthquake that threatened to burst the hollow cave. But Hercules did not slow his run until he felt his face collide with pelt, his hands tangle in the long-haired mane and his knees clamp shut around the glassy hindquarters.

Half strangling, half hanging on, he felt the gigantic

artery beat in the beast's foam-flecked neck. He felt the spinal cord through its beastly hide. He twisted and he wrung and he ground and he pounded until the lion—the terror of Nemea—flapped like a rug, and its flexing hide gave off a cloud of dust and fleas.

He skinned it and he scraped the skin. He tore off his own clothes, spattered with his own children's blood, and he put on the lion's pelt instead.

A city guard stared down from the wall of Argos and called timidly, 'Who goes there? Man or beast?'

Hercules silenced him with a scowl, and hurried on into the king's palace. Over his shoulders hung the velvet forepaws of the Nemean Lion, and across his forehead snarled the jawless, velvet nose. Its tasselled tail dragged in the dust behind him, and the pelt rippled across his back as he moved. The hind paws of the skin were knotted around his waist and dangled past his knees.

King Eurystheus was just finishing his breakfast when the door opened and a lion, walking rampant on its hind legs and wearing a human face, strolled in on him. The head lunged forward: Hercules was bowing.

When the servants found King Eurystheus, they could not persuade him to open the wardrobe door for fully half an hour. His little voice piped through the latch, 'Tell him to go away . . . Tell him to go and . . . Tell him . . . ' The latch clacked back, and Eurystheus's snub nose wiffled through a tiny gap. 'Tell him to go and kill the Hydra!'

4

Two Heads are Better than a Hundred

'We all know what Hera is doing,' said Hermes, in a hushed but angry voice. He was sitting cross-legged on a brush-covered slope of Olympus, surrounded by others of the Immortals who looked sulky and peevish. The cloud layer which screened the topmost peaks of the mountain from being glimpsed by earthly mortals, fumed and churned above their bent heads, and the air was clammy with water vapour. The gods were hiding.

Well, perhaps they were not exactly hiding, which would not have been dignified, but they were holding their meeting well out of sight of the queen's eyes.

'It's cruel,' said Athene.

'It's uncharitable,' said Apollo.

'And it's against a son of Zeus-the-Almighty,' said Hermes, 'which is more to the point. All in all, I'd rather be on the side of Hercules, if Zeus finds out what his wife is up to.'

'It's malicious,' said Athene.

'It's spiteful,' said Apollo.

'And it puts us gods in a poor light if the mortals hear

about it,' said Hermes, 'which they undoubtedly will. If Hercules kills the Hydra, it will be the talk of the world.'

'Well, I'll give my archer's bow,' said Apollo.

'And I'll give my sword,' said Hermes.

'And I'll give my helmet,' said Athene. 'He's got the skin of the Nemean Lion to protect his body.'

So softly, silently they went down to the base of Olympus, and furtively placed the weapons on Hercules's path to the Hydra's lair. Well, perhaps they did not do it furtively, for that would not have been dignified.

But when Hercules found the helmet and sword and bow, and looked up at heaven with a beaming smile, and bawled, *Thank you, my lords and ladies!'*, all that came back was a startling buffet of breezes: 'SHSHSH!', and a creaking in the trees that sounded like, 'Hera will hear you! Hera will hear!'

The Lernean swamps writhed with the roots of drowned trees, and things squirmed unseen underfoot in the black mud. 'I don't like it,' said Iolaus.

Hercules had called in on his friend, Iolaus, who lived not very far from the lair of the Hydra. It had occurred to the strong man of Thebes that he might well meet his death in the Lernean swamp, and he did not want it thought that he had simply run away—disappeared out of cowardice. 'All you have to do is to watch, and report back to Eurystheus . . . if I . . . if the Hydra gets the better of me.'

'Gets the better of you?' squeaked Iolaus, his eyes bulging with horror. 'Have you ever *seen* the Hydra? Do you have any idea what you're talking about? It's . . . it's . . . it's so horrible that people fall down and die at the mere sight of it! Cut off one head and two grow in its place. It must have twelve heads by now, at least! I've lived in these parts all my life—it's safe enough outside the swamp—but I've seen the "heroes", so-called, piling in here to do great battle—all set to be famous.' He reached out and clutched his friend's arm. 'They none of them came out again, Hercules! I heard the screams. I heard the Hydra whistle. And every time, the whistle gets louder!'

Hercules slapped at the mosquitos which swarmed up off the water in clouds. 'Now, now, Iolaus, don't take it so much to heart. You know I'm not chasing fame. I'd rather be at home in bed. But the gods bound me to serve Eurystheus, and Eurystheus told me to kill the Hydra. So. Here we are. Don't let me down. Who was it used to eat spiders and keep a pet ragworm when we were young? Don't tell me you've grown squeamish all of a sudden?'

Beyond the next tree, Hercules almost trod on a sleeping head of the Hydra.

Like a gigantic python it was, though many of its teeth protruded through the thick, scaly lips. Without a second thought, Hercules drew his new, unblooded sword, and cut through the reptilian neck.

Instead of blood, a resinous gum welled in the wound—welled and swelled and formed a skin like scalded milk; swelled and healed and formed a green-pointed fork; welled and swelled until the forked ends bulged like rosehips with two new, born-blind heads. Both heads snarled. In both mouths, the teeth were already grown. And a spine-chilling whistle came from the nostrils on every outward breath.

Many more heroes must have fought the Hydra since Iolaus calculated the number of its heads. For now it had at least a hundred—a wilderness of swaying tendrils, and on the end of every tendril a vile, reptilian head. Like a squid or a great, fronded sea-plant disturbed by a turning tide, the Hydra quivered, and all its eyes opened.

The swamp in which it was rooted was clogged with rags and bones and hair, as the grass is below an owl's tree—the regurgitated waste from many, many meals. The heads ducked and weaved: it was impossible to count them, for they all looked alike, and all gaped mouths with banks of needle-sharp, thorn-black teeth and pulsating, soft, red palates. The whistle grew almost deafening.

The mouths lunged at Hercules. He was slow to jump backwards, and two pairs of jaws closed on his body. But the teeth could not penetrate the thick hide of the Nemean Lion. They stayed clenched in the fur when he cut through the necks with his sword. Four new heads were soon swaying among the forest of heads. He cut off six more. Twelve new heads were soon darting at him, and the fur of his lionskin was bitten bald. He backed away, stumbling in the quagmire, and joined Iolaus behind the shelter of a tree. The whistling and the tendrils pursued him, but the jaws could not reach so far.

Iolaus stared at him: 'You're alive! Pick up a head or two, stuff them in a sack and take them back to Argos. The king will think the Hydra's dead.'

Hercules, panting and leaning his back against the tree, looked shocked. 'But that would be dishonest! I couldn't hide the truth from the gods, could I? The gods would know. No, no, it's all right . . . I have a plan. Light a fire.'

Difficult as that was in the middle of a swamp, Iolaus looked on fire-lighting as simplicity itself compared with killing the Hydra. He scurried about, piling twigs into a hollow tree, and raised a fire as big as a beacon, thinking that Hercules wanted to summon help.

Not a bit of it. Into the fire Hercules thrust his massive club which was cut from such dense, massy wood that it glowed white hot and charred without burning up. 'Now. Every time I bring you an end, seal it with the club.'

'*What!*' shrieked Iolaus. But Hercules had gone. He was in among the thrashing Hydra's hundred and fifty heads like a man embroiled in octopus, reaching for the air and drowning . . .

But Hercules did not drown. Nor did the Hydra's heads chew him into a quid of lion fur, hair, and sandal. Its heads flew like the ears of corn under a flail, and two-at-a-time Hercules heaved the cut tendrils away from the rest. Like a stevedore drags the massive cables of a ship to the bollard, he hauled them to where Iolaus stood holding the glowing club.

'Well, don't just stand there, man! Seal the ends!' And Iolaus shut his eyes and held out the club (which took all his strength). There was a terrible noise of sizzling, and a smell of roasting lizard. The whole Hydra writhed and whistled.

But the cauterized necks did not grow new heads, and little by little Hercules hacked his way through the beast like a woodsman through a thicket: hacked and branded, hacked and branded, until the Hydra stood, like a pollarded willow beside a stream, stock still.

The whole swamp seemed suddenly to be shrinking, as if its putrid acres had sprung directly from the foot of the Hydra. A million slimy creatures from out of the mud were exposed to the purging heat of the sun.

One creature lay still as a stone. Very like a stone it was, with its rosy-white, hinged back. And while its legs were still submerged beneath the swamp, anyone might have trodden on it for a stepping stone. Hercules was about to do just that, in his haste to get back to Argos with the news of his conquest. He was not cautious about where he trod.

'Look out!' It was Iolaus who spotted the huge, serrated claw rising out of the water and the eight hinged legs. It was a huge land-crab.

Hercules drew back his foot. The crab sank down beneath the last layers of muddy water. But its two stalked eyes still waved in the air, watching him. With undreamt-of speed the eye-stalks moved through the fetid water as the crab scuttled in to bite. It was not to be robbed of its meat.

So Hercules plunged his club, still glowing hot, into the swamp, and the water round about it again steamed and hissed. Blushing pink with the heat, the crab bobbed up to the surface and escaped by scuttering sideways up a tree trunk. When it was on a level with Hercules's head, it flung itself at his throat, pincers gaping.

Iolaus squealed and put his arms over his head. Hercules swung his club and hit the crab in mid-air as though it was a bowled ball.

It cracked like the fossilized egg of some prehistoric monster, and something akin to its yolk dribbled out where it landed. The plants round about sizzled and burned with the foulest of smells, and both men covered their faces against the smoke. The land-crab's great claw clutched and wavered once, then fell.

Naturally curious to study such a huge specimen, Hercules went and poked at the dead crab with one of his arrows. The arrowhead went quite black before he put it back into its quiver.

'It's been good to see you again after all this time,' said Hercules to Iolaus. 'Thank you for your help. Don't let's leave it so long until we meet again.'

Iolaus looked back to that muddy spot where he had stood fully expecting to die. 'Well, Hercules, old friend, you know me. If ever you need anyone to help you out like this again, do me a favour . . . *ask someone else*!'

* * *

When they told King Eurystheus that Hercules had been sighted from the city wall—and with helmet, sword, and bow—he ran three times round his throne. 'Go and fetch it! Go and fetch it now! Go and fetch my box!' he jabbered, and his slaves ran from the room. They could be heard struggling down the corridor with some very great weight. 'Set it down! Set it down! Set it down!'

They were only just in time. Hercules was at the door before Eurystheus slammed shut the lid of his newly wrought, great brass chest.

'Hail, master and cousin. The Hydra is d—' Hercules stopped and looked around. The king did not seem to be in the room.

'Dead, you say? Don't believe it!'

Hercules looked again round the room, but there was no sign of the king. An embarrassed slave jerked his head once or twice in the direction of a huge brass chest standing beside the throne. Two slits halfway down, and in the slits the glitter of two eyes, revealed the presence of King Eurystheus. Hercules looked to the slave for an explanation, but the boy only shrugged as if to say, 'Don't ask me.'

Unsure of the correct protocol for addressing a king sealed up in a big brass box, Hercules sidled up to it with some embarrassment, and knelt down respectfully on one knee. Like that, he was on a level to peer through the slits. The eyes inside blinked, and a little whimper escaped the trunk.

'The Hydra really is dead. Send someone to see,' said Hercules in a friendly way. 'It's easy to find what's left, now that the swamp has dried up.'

A sigh of vexation echoed round the chest. 'Wait there, slave. I'm thinking.' The eyes disappeared from the

34

slits, and the flicker of a candle licked yellow. There was a rustle of vellum documents, and pause enough for Hercules to look about. He noticed that there were charts and maps stuck to every wall of the throne-room with wax. He got up and went to examine them. Cerynia . . . Erymanthus . . . Elis . . . Crete . . . Stymphalus . . .

'I have another task for—Where have you gone?' said the box. Hercules ran back and knelt in front of it. 'I have another task for you, slave. Fetch me the Golden Stag of Cerynia.'

'What, dead?' said Hercules rather sadly. The Hydra and the lion had been one thing, but to kill the beautiful Stag of Cerynia seemed an awful waste.

Eurystheus, thinking to make the task even more impossible, said, 'No! Alive! Bring it to me alive!'

'Oh that's all right, then,' muttered Hercules with relief, and was immediately gone, leaving the brass chest delivering a pompous speech to no one at all except for a shuffling, uneasy slave.

5

Big Game and Sore Losses

For a year he trailed through the forests of Cerynia without ever a sighting. Sometimes he thought he heard its bronze hooves clatter against the dead branches that lay like snares under the fallen leaves. But it was only a woodpecker hammering at a tree. Sometimes he thought he caught sight of its golden antlers rattling the branches. But it was only the glancing rays of a low sun glimpsed through the crooked tree-tops. Sometimes he ran after its dappled hide only to find that he was chasing the spotted sunlight across the forest floor. And once he dreamt that a velvet lip nuzzled against his face, and woke to find spoors and hoofprints. But the stag had gone.

So finally he fetched salt from the shore of the sea, and carried it to all the pools of the forest but one. And he poured the salt into the pools until their taste was brackish and foul, and little frogs scuttered away through the green woods.

Only one fresh pool was left, and beside it he sat down with his back to a tree and his net in a bundle beside him, and he waited. For three days he waited, and the animals of the forest all came by him, panting for fresh water after drinking saltwater elsewhere. Squirrels and wild cats, roebuck and birds, rats and boars all brushed past him, some cautious, some reckless, but paying him no attention at all until their thirst was quenched. Hercules nodded and dozed.

There was frost on the ground when it came, and there was no mistaking the sound of its coming. All the other animals had drunk and gone, drunk and hidden from the cold. The pool was deserted. Its bronze hooves clashed on the frozen water with the sound of cymbals, and its golden horns rang as they shook the frozen reeds. Its hide sparkled with frost.

Having drunk at one of the salted ponds, the Golden Stag was parched for fresh water. It kicked and trampled on the ice that encrusted the water, and half-fell, half-leapt knee-deep into the shallow pool. Hercules opened his eyes the merest flicker, and his heart beat fast at the sheer beauty of the stag. But he did not move so much as a finger, for fear of frightening it away. He could see the sparkling throat gulp down the icy water and its warm breath turn to steam. Hercules's right hand crept towards his nets, like a spider crawling towards its web.

The creature heard the little grunt driven from Hercules's throat by the effort of the throw. It might have bounded, straight-legged, out of the far side of the pond but for the treacherous ice. It stumbled a little, and that was enough for the whistling net to overshadow it, then fall over the golden antlers and the glittering rump. Hercules leapt into the icy pool, and drawing close the rim of the net round the stag's knees, he bent his back and lifted the animal, his arms encircling all its four spindly legs. Like a stoop of golden corn he held it up high, and felt it tremble in his arms as he waded and slithered up the icy bank again. His own body began to tremble with the cold. Deer and man shook as though they were one beast.

Now at last Hercules could see that the antlers were not metal at all, but coated in a golden sheen of blooming velvet. In spring the gold would slough away. And the hooves were not made of bronze. They were only stained to a bronzy ochre by the oils of vetches and fleshy daisies it had trampled underfoot. The precious glitter of its coat thawed in the heat of fear, and ran down over Hercules's arms: water.

The stag was the most beautiful creature in the Cerynian Forest, but once inside the treasure house of a king it would be no more than a square of vellum, a pot of glue, a meal or two of venison.

'I shall take you to Eurystheus,' said Hercules softly, into one of the swivelling, flickering ears, 'but I'm afraid you'll be a sorry disappointment to him.'

'Take him to Eurystheus, will you? Not *my* deer you won't,' said a woman's voice. A pack of dogs bounded barking into the grove. Hercules shifted the stag this way and that in his arms and twisted his head round until he could see who was speaking. And he saw a woman, dressed in a doeskin tunic, holding a bow at full stretch, its arrow aimed at his back.

Hercules sighed. 'Does this fellow belong to you?' he asked, rocking the deer in his arms. It had ceased to struggle, and rested its jaw on the top of his head to look at the woman out of its golden, blinking eyes, through the mesh of the net.

'Why wouldn't he?' snapped the woman. 'Aren't I Artemis, immortal goddess of the hunt?'

'Oh. I see. Do you want me to let him go, then, madam?'

Artemis did not answer questions. She asked them, pouncingly, like a cat asking a mouse whether it wants to play. 'Explanation! What's your explanation? Who are you?'

'I'm Hercules of Thebes. I was sent to catch the Stag of Cerynia by my cousin, King Eurystheus.'

'You? Why you? Explanation!'

'Because I'm his bond-slave . . . Look, you put down the bow and I'll put down the stag. The gods set me to these labours, and if a goddess takes my prize from me, I know it must be my fate. What's a wasted year?'

The dogs bounding and barking round Hercules and snapping at the Golden Stag, struck a new terror into the animal and it began to struggle and kick. Hercules stumbled to and fro, surrounded by swarming dogs, the deer's antlers rattling the tree branches overhead.

'Labours? Gods? Which gods? Explanation!' snapped Artemis, striding about, drawing and easing her bow. A quiver of arrows worn diagonally across her back, pinned into place a torrent of red-gold hair longer than her tunic. The arrows were fletched with the feathers of birds Hercules had never seen. He heaved a weary sigh as he thought of Eurystheus's gloating spite when his bond-slave returned empty-handed. He had failed, after a year's patient effort. Surely Artemis, as one of the Immortals, knew of the doom carved by fire in the walls of Thebes. He was loath to tell the story of his crime again. But she insisted.

'I am Hercules, son of Alcmene and foster son of King Amphitryon of Thebes . . .'

By the time he finished, the goddess Artemis was sitting on a heap of panting, tail-wagging dogs, her chin in her hands, gazing up at Hercules who was still holding the Golden Stag. 'Go on,' she said, when he paused.

'There's nothing else to say. King Eurystheus commanded me to kill the Nemean Lion and the Hydra, and now he wants the Golden Stag of Cerynia.'

'That's the saddest story I ever heard,' said Artemis,

and tears streamed picturesquely down her suntanned face. The dogs whimpered obediently. 'I haven't been back to Olympus recently. I didn't know. I think someone up there must really hate you, and I can guess who. I mean I've only got to look at you to see whose son *you* are. He's a little bigger, of course. Almighty Zeus is a bit bigger.'

The stag had gone to sleep in Hercules's arms. It flinched and stirred as Hercules burst out laughing. 'Oh yes! Very likely! Me, the son of Zeus! And who's to blame for my sufferings except me? *I* drank myself to a madness, didn't I? *I* slaughtered my wife and kin, didn't I? No punishment is bad enough for me. I wonder what Eurystheus will do to me when I go back without the stag.'

Artemis looked at him with her head on one side. 'What strange creatures you mortals are. If we gods had to pay for our crimes, we'd spend from now till the end of time breaking rocks on the bottom of the sea. Off you go. The stag's yours—just so long as it's set free afterwards. But you know, its antlers aren't gold. And its hooves aren't bronze.'

'I see that,' said Hercules, hitching up the burden in his arms. 'I'm sure when my cousin sees that, he will be perfectly content for the beast to go free.'

Artemis wiped the tears off her face with a length of her hair. As she got up off her couch of dogs, they bounded madly this way and that, and woke up the stag again and sent Hercules stumbling to and fro with its struggles. When he looked round next, Artemis and all her dogs had gone. All the ice had melted off the pool, and primroses had burst into flower among the tree roots.

King Eurystheus was not impressed with the Golden Stag

of Cerynia. Confronted with a large, nervous stag, taller than his throne and clattering its oily feet on the marble floor, he climbed into his brass chest again and shut the lid.

Hercules waited for a time, and when the king did not come out again or shout any instructions through the slits, he went and referred to the maps on the wall. In the centre of a map of the province of Erymanthus, he saw a picture of a huge pig with tusks. 'Should I go after this next?' asked Hercules loudly.

The boy-slave in attendance by the throne could not keep silent. 'Oh yes! Please do, Hercules sir! My family lives in Erymanthus and the boar is the terror of the world. If anyone can kill it, you can! We all have faith in you! Oh please go there next!'

The lid clanged back on the brass box, and King Eurystheus poked out his head. 'Where's Hercules gone?' he demanded to know.

'He's gone to kill the Erymanthean Boar, sir,' said the slave-boy, dropping to his knees.

'Oh. Oh good. Good . . . Is it *very* dangerous?'

'Desperately dangerous, sire.'

'Excellent. Be sure to tell me if he gets killed. Now take that worthless hoax of a deer and turn it into venison. Look what it's doing now!'

They led it away, its bony antlers rattling the lamps overhead. But, without warning, it sprang through a high window, and disappeared amid the damp sheen of the gardens. Later it could be seen sometimes at the far end of a promenade or behind the fruit trees, its antler-velvet glistening like gold and its oily hooves shining like bronze, and granules of frost glistening like gems in its winter coat.

* * *

41

When Hercules crushed the giant land-crab in the swamp of the Hydra, the squelch was heard in heaven. Hera, lying full length along a lintel of lazuli, gouged at her couch like a cat sharpening its claws. 'Oh you villain, Hercules. You blood-thirsty, heartless wretch. What have you done to my Cancer, my darling little crab, my purveyor of poison, my deliverer of death? What, little one, are you dead and your work not done? One scratch of your poisonous claw would have sent Hercules screaming to his grave! Should I forgive you for failing me? No, you worthless object. But see what a funeral I shall give you.'

And she sent an eagle to fetch the crab's body from the swamp. She toyed with the dead thing for a moment, then hurled it over the horizon into the night beyond. As the sun sank, and night wheeled over the tree-tops to take possession of the sky, there hung the crab, cut out in stars, for all eternity. Falling stars dropped from between its spreading claws; like green drops of venom they drip-drip-dripped on to the Earth, though no one could say where they fell.

'Dear Cancer! Your venom is black on Hercules's arrowhead,' whispered Hera. 'Now let the sweet droplets of your revenge fall on his head and on the heads of those he loves. You shall hang in the sky for ever as a mark of my hatred for Hercules!'

6

Poisons

Hercules hoped for an easy conquest over the Erymanthean Boar—not because it was any less fierce than the Nemean Lion, but because its territory was the homeland of the centaurs. He resolved to go and visit his one-time games-master and ask his advice. So he approached their mountain home across the wintry plain, calling Chiron's name until he was half-hoarse. But he saw neither hide nor hair of his friend.

Then at last he caught sight of him, in a break in the trees, on the brow of Arcadia's hills. Hercules raised his hand and waved—and Chiron shied away on to the far side of the peak. There was no catching up with him.

The centaur's strange behaviour cast a bleak shadow over Hercules. He was bitterly cold; it was starting to snow, and he had not slept indoors since he began his bondage to Eurystheus. The prospect of another night under the frost-sharpened stars, curled up on the frost-sharpened ground, seemed suddenly insupportable. So he searched the hillside until he found a cave and, announcing his name on the threshold, he ducked inside, into the warmth of the centaurs' hearth.

'Greetings, Hercules. We have all heard a great deal about you. Come in, come in. Eat with us tonight, and sleep in the warm.' The only occupant of the cave was Pholus, whose hooves were large and hairy, and whose upper body had a fat, round belly as pink as onyx. He was cooking a meal of peas and beans in two large cauldrons. The other centaurs were still out on the hill, hunting or competing in games, keeping a wary look-out for the Erymanthean Boar which had killed seven of their number already.

Hercules sat down. 'I think I saw Chiron earlier. Will he come back here this evening?'

Pholus dropped his spoon with a clatter, and took a long time retrieving it. He was clearly embarrassed. 'No. I don't suppose so. Not if he knows you're here.'

'But he's an old friend! He taught me sports, you know. I'm a pupil of his . . .'

'Oh yes. He's told us all about you, Hercules. We know all about you. I'm an easy-going old hack, myself. But Chiron . . . well, Chiron's different. When he heard what happened at Thebes, he just . . . well, he just somehow . . .'

'Of course! He knows I broke my promise!' Hercules clapped his hands to his head and groaned. 'I must speak to him. He has to forgive me! You must help me to find him!'

Pholus tasted the dinner and stared thoughtfully at the roof, clearly struggling to find the least offensive words. 'I'm sure he forgives you, Hercules. It's just that he's *afraid* of you, you see.'

'*Afraid?*'

'We try to tell him it was a silly mistake. One silly mistake. But all he ever says is, ''A man who drinks once will drink twice.'' So, you see, I don't think Chiron will come in tonight.'

Hercules was stunned. He was choked with sorrow; he was furiously angry. Could Chiron seriously think that, having lost a wife and children because of wine, Hercules would drink again? Did he really trust his pupil so little? Hercules was wounded. 'Does he think that he has more will-power than I have? He doesn't drink! I won't drink!'

'*Chiron not drink?* Whatever gave you that idea,' said Pholus with a hinny. 'He *tries* not to. But every so often—when he's really down—back he goes to the vat. We centaurs are all alike. Drink's in our blood, and when we drink, there's a thousand years of civilization washed away in the flood. We chase women, we fall off mountains, we walk on to the tusks of the Erymanthean Boar. Centaurs will always be centaurs, no matter how much Chiron would like us to change.'

Hercules's head sank lower and lower between his knees. He had come to the centaurs' cave for comfort, and now he was more wretched than ever. Chiron drink? Chiron afraid of his own pupil? The hero of his childhood suddenly seemed small and flawed—a disappointment. All he had ever taught Hercules was thrown into doubt.

He brooded and brooded, and while he brooded, Pholus set a splendid meal of hot peas and beans and a whole loaf of warm bread at the guest's feet, along with a jug of milk.

'What, no wine?' said Hercules sarcastically.

Pholus blushed. 'Ah. The wine's not mine to offer, sir. It's the property of the centaur tribe. On the feast of Bacchus we do take the odd . . . '

'I want some!' said Hercules, pushing his face into Pholus's face. 'Now! Chiron says, "If a man drinks once, he'll drink twice".'

Then Pholus blenched. 'No, sir. Chiron's a fool, sir. You mustn't take to heart what he says. He's never

45

spoken a sensible word in his life. We laughed at him. We threw crusts at him. "Hercules is wise now," we all said.'

Hercules caught him by the beard. 'Are you calling my old friend a fool? Let me tell you something! I used to love Chiron like a brother. He was clever. He was fit. He was wise. If he says I'll drink a second time, then that's what I'll do. And I'll do it now. *So give me some wine!*'

'No!' said Pholus. 'No! No! No! I won't bring wine to you. We all know what happened last time!' And he cantered out of the cave, a paunchy, ungainly beast snorting down both nostrils.

Hercules walked up to the vat and smashed a hole in it with one blow of his fist. A geyser of wine struck him in the face, and he had only to open his mouth to drink.

It was made from fruit grown on the foothills of Paradise, but it tasted bitter, because he was drinking to get even with Chiron, and because he loved Chiron, and for a host of angry reasons in between. The vat spewed its contents down his chest and legs, and flooded the floor of the cave.

Meanwhile Pholus ran for help. He shouted, 'Come quick, the strong man is here! Chiron's Hercules is drinking the wine! Someone! Come quickly! Hercules is drinking! Chiron! Hercules is drinking again!'

Chiron, who had been creeping closer and closer to the cave in the hope of seeing his pupil once more from a distance, lost all fear at the sound of Pholus's voice. He only knew that he had to stop Hercules—that something terrible would happen if Hercules ever again allowed wine to wash away his senses. Through the thick, evening undergrowth he bolted, no slower on his feet than when he had taught steeplechasing to the Prince of Thebes.

But he was too late to stop Hercules from drinking. By the time he reached the cave, the stars were sparkling overhead like the bubbles in a dark, rich wine, and in the doorway of the cave Hercules stood swaying, his Olympian bow and arrow clutched like a lute, his eyes bloodshot like wine-fermented cheese.

'Hercules! Ho there! It's I!' cried Chiron.

Hercules peered through a darkness thickened to syrup by the fumes of drink, and saw a low tossing of the undergrowth. 'You, eh? I've been looking for you these five days past.'

So Chiron hurried on towards Hercules and stretched out his arms by way of greeting and apology. He was only a few paces away when Hercules raised his bow and fired.

Chiron leapt. The champion of the high jump leapt straight up into the air, twisting his head away and drawing up his long, slender legs. But the arrow struck him in the fetlock, and he fell on his side, and his tail shrouded the bushes with strands of silk. Pholus saw it all.

'There!' said Hercules. '*He* won't be troubling you any more. I've killed the Erymanthean Boar for you. Saw it. Shot it. Just like that. Piaow!' And he slid down the cave wall and slumped along the ground, insensible with drink. The last thing he saw, as he rolled over and his mouth fell open, was the constellation of Cancer the Crab dripping its starlight on to the hill of the centaurs.

Pholus ran to the side of his brother centaur. 'Chiron! Chiron! Let me help you! Let me see that wound!'

Chiron had his two hands clutched below his withers, and his legs twitched and kicked in agony. Pholus knelt down and pulled out the arrow. Its head was not shiny, but black and corroded. He tested its sharpness against his thumb and cut himself. For a moment he stared at

47

the little cut, and then he clutched his upper arm and said, 'Always clumsy. Always clumsy and stupid, that's me.' He gave a little sob, then rolled over, with his head in the angle of Chiron's body, and died.

Next morning, Hercules's head felt like a foul and overheated kitchen, where pots and pans hung from the ceiling and clattered and banged against each other. A scream came howling through the kitchen, setting the pans swinging and banging, swinging and banging. Hercules opened his eyes.

On the hillside, the whole tribe of centaurs was ranged in a ring around Chiron and the body of Pholus. Chiron was standing on his hind horses' legs, pawing the air with his front hooves and tearing at his mane of hair with both hands. Then he flung himself down on his back and clutched his wounded leg, and thrashed his hind flanks and heaved his upper body along the ground as though he were trying to pull man from horse. He called over and over again on the gods.

The centaurs would hardly make way for Hercules. They landed furtive kicks on him as he pushed his way through to Chiron. His sports-master stared at him with rolling eyes: even his upper body was creamy with sweat, like a horse. 'Well, boy, and who taught you to poison your arrows?'

'Poison? Arrows? Chiron, what have I done to you?'

'You've condemned me to everlasting torment, boy! Pholus was lucky—he wasn't an immortal like me. But me! I can't die! I can't be rid of the pain that's breeding and multiplying inside me like a million horseflies! Did I deserve this? For telling you the truth? Oh, Hercules! Pray to the gods to let me die like an ordinary mortal!'

Then Hercules saw the black-headed arrow and remembered the swamp and the Hydra and the land-crab and the hanging constellation oozing starlight. 'Me? Pray?' he said. 'Why would the gods pay any heed to a man who kills his friends?' and he embraced the half-man that was Chiron. When he broke free again, he turned his face to the sky and howled, 'If it's true, what Artemis said in the woods of Cerynia—if it is true that Almighty Zeus is my father, I ask one thing and one thing only for my birthright. Take this my friend, as someone took that foul crab, and scatter him in stars on the night sky as a glory to his race. And make him of stars so bright that they will prick my eyes each night and make me weep!'

Seizing the centaur by its horses' heels, he swung and loosed him like a folded sling, and hurled him upwards into the sky. The clouds shook with howling. And the lesser gods, who had been watching all the time, caught and carried him far out into the fields of night where other beasts graze on the periwinkle stars. And there they parted him, as the sun's rays are parted, when they strike the sea, into scattering drops of light. And there, in the cold of space, the droplets froze, each containing the essence of Chiron, his energy and intellect and wild centaurian fire.

Not until the following night did Hercules see his friend rear up over the hill of the centaurs, with a bow of moonlight and a quiver of meteorites, as though he were hunting constellar beasts across the night sky.

Pholus he buried in the hillside, in frost-hard clay, in a grave that was instantly covered by falling snow. During the blizzard, Hercules picked up his weapons and left. The centaurs did not see him go.

He followed the tracks of the Erymanthean Boar quite easily; the snow was as deep as the beast's bristling underbelly and it picked out a laborious path. He found it sleeping, and wrapped it in a net. Then he took it back to Argos, hog-tied, and set it down in front of Eurystheus's brass hidey-hole.

'You see what a kindness I've done you, cousin Hercules,' piped the king shrilly. 'The world talks of nothing but Hercules and his great labours. Not a word about your master. Not a word about *me*. I'm not sure I ought to give you any more of these opportunities to show off. I'm not sure I shouldn't lock you in a dungeon somewhere until the world forgets that you were ever born. I'm not sure a child murderer deserves such fame. I hear you've been killing centaurs this time. Another friend of yours dead, eh? It hardly benefits a man to call himself your friend, does it? I'm glad I can only claim to be your master, your owner, your better . . . '

'You are what you are,' mumbled Hercules, grinding his teeth. 'I am obedient to whatever work you give me. But I beg you, cousin, let my next task be more of a hardship and less of a glory, and let it be work enough to make me sleep at night. I have things in my head that don't bear remembering.'

The box gave a gulp. 'Well, take that pig away and have it roasted, and then be on your way to Elis. The smell of the place begins to offend my realm. There'll be no glory to reap from *this* labour, just work enough to keep you labouring for ten years, and filth enough to bury your pride. I'm lending you to Augeas to clean out his stables!'

An eerie laugh trickled in at the threshold. And though panic-stricken servants set about it with brooms, to sweep it out again, it got in behind the furniture, and came out at night, like mice, to gnaw on the silence. *'You have done well,'* Hera's voice whispered to Eurystheus from behind his curtains as he undressed. *'This labour is much the best of all, my little man!'* And a clammy hand touched him in the small of the back before he could pull the covers close round him.

50

7

Mucking Out

King Augeas had farm animals more than he could count. When they were loosed into the meadows they blotted out the landscape as far as the horizon—a great landmass of goats and bullocks and horses, overhung by clouds of flies. At nightfall, they were driven, with whips and whistles, into a stable that stretched for mile upon granite mile, over the horizon and beyond. They were sent as tributes by the kingdom's frightened neighbours—bribes offered in the hope of sweetening his barbarous temper. But nothing could sweeten the stables themselves.

Once Augeas had sent his slaves into the stables in droves to clean out the dirty straw, but the animals' trampling hooves and close-squeezing flanks had crushed them, and their bones lay lost beneath fifty years of dung.

To walk into the smell was like walking into a wall. All the beasts were diseased, and their ribs stood out like whip-weals, and their eyes were ringed with madness at the neglect that had blighted their lives.

King Augeas moved his bed further and further away from the stables, to the backmost rooms, then the leeward gardens, until at last a broad mountain stood between him and the stinking valley. He no longer troubled to loose the animals into the meadows, but left them penned up, day and night. The squalor disgusted even him.

Eurystheus did send a messenger ahead of Hercules. But as the messenger came up the valley and caught wind of the stables, he gave one sniff and ran away. So Hercules himself had to explain the task that had been set him. The king's couch was resting now between banks of hydrangea bushes with an awning to keep off the rain. He was dressed in a loose robe which had once been thickly embroidered with gold thread. But since he never troubled to undress by night or change his clothes in the morning, the garment had grown worse than shabby. It looked like a fisherman's net hung up to dry with a few ragged fish still dangling in the mesh. Night and day he lay reclining on his couch and eating, and vultures perched on the bedhead and ate his leftovers off the covers.

When he heard why Hercules had come, he rolled on to his back like a dog, and laughed chokingly. The honking giggle caused him great discomfort because of the wedges of wax he had used to stop up his nose against the smell. 'I'll make a wager with you, boy. Never mind Eurystheus. Never mind slavery. If you can clean out my stables, you can keep half the beasts yourself. And that's the word of a man who's never given away so much as a cold in the head.'

'I accept, Augeas. I accept your wager,' said Hercules. 'Now, if you could show me the stables?'

'Show you? Huh! I'm sure you can nose them out yourself. I'm not stirring a step in *that* direction.'

Hercules could see a thundercloud of flies hanging beyond the mountain. He could hear their buzzing. As he walked down into the valley of the stables, it was snowing flies, hailing flies. His feet sank into the boggy moss of the mountainside and at once swarms of flies gathered to drink the water that filled his footprints.

If the flies were thirsty, the animals were parched. A little choked stream which trickled alongside the stables kept alive those that could reach it, stretching their scraggy necks through the holes in the stable wall. Others, hollow-eyed, were dying of thirst. When Hercules threw open the doors, they had hardly enough strength to stumble out and jostle for a lick of water. League upon league of fly-blown creatures came wading through years of dung, out into the valley meadows. The light troubled them. The flies persecuted them. Hercules ached with pity. He threw down his pitchfork, and scratched the ears of a goat-kid that came and nuzzled his hand. The task was plainly impossible. A man could work a lifetime and still be ankle-deep in dung. In despair, he walked the entire length of the valley, and the little kid followed on behind him, until the sound of fast-flowing water tempted it away over a hill crest. Then Hercules followed the kid instead.

He found himself looking down at a raging river full of splintered tree trunks and scouring sand. Froth ringed all the rocks with a white and delicate lace.

'Water,' said Hercules. 'Clean, running water!'

At the water's edge on the far side of the river, crouched a young man scrubbing his body with a knot of wet grass. His skin gleamed and glowed, but his hands were red and wrinkled with being too much in water. Beyond him, a second, slow, green river made a meandering loop so as almost to maroon him on a dry spit of land between the two strands of water. He started at the sight of Hercules, and his twist of grass tumbled away downstream.

In a feverish burst of activity, Hercules set about

tearing up light rocks from the river bank and pitching them into the water: boulders and logs and whole trees and yet more boulders, until the debris washing down the swollen river began to pile up against his dam. The more it piled up, the more solid the dam grew, until the river began to spill over its bank and grope icily at Hercules's feet. The astonished youth washing himself on the far shore made a snatch at the river as though it were a coverlet slipping off his bed. But the river escaped his clutch. It was re-routing itself.

Hercules scraped a path for it with a tree branch. He rolled boulders out of its way. He diverted it into the valley of the Augean stables.

The beasts looked up from their grazing, from beneath their blanket of flies, and their eyes rolled with fear. For pouring down the valley came a rushing river, bounding and pounding across the mired grass and crowning each obstacle with foam. It chased them on to high ground: it washed their mildewed hooves.

It crashed against the stable doors and spouted in at the few small windows. It swirled through the stalls as dawn scours the sea-lanes with her first rays. It sluiced away the dirt like time sluices the present into the past.

Only when it was dangerously deep and threatened to sweep Hercules off his feet, did he wade against the current and throw down the dam he had built. The river returned to its usual course, roaring angrily like a beast disturbed from its sleep. Up on the hilltop, the young man was dancing and flinging his hands over his head and yelping with joy.

Dipping puzzled noses into the receding water, the beasts watched the water gurgle and suck and soak away. The stable building stood as white as the temples glimpsed on sunlit mountaintops. Its roofs were torn or sagging; the mangers were all piled up against the end wall where the water had swept them. Dispossessed flies teamed down the valley, mourning their comfortable dung, and here and there white stones gleamed like a trail of coins dropped from the pocket of a passing giant.

'It's done,' said Hercules. He had to say it twice before Augeas woke up.

'What do you take me for?'

'I tell you it's done.'

The king took the wax out of his nose and sniffed—gingerly at first and then deeper and deeper.

'Look for yourself,' said Hercules.

For an hour Augeas sat at the head of the valley and stared. No flicker of joy touched his unshaven face. At last he said, 'Look at it. The roof's all smashed.'

'That's soon mended,' said Hercules, rather taken aback.

'It's a ruin.'

'It was a ruin when I got here!'

'You youngsters. No patience to do a job properly. Always the quick trick, the slick trick. How did you do it?'

'He diverted the rivers, father! He drove rivers through there like a herd of horses. In half a day, he did it! Fifty years of filth in half a day!' It was the well-washed and shiny-faced boy from beside the river.

Augeas turned on them both a look of vilest contempt. 'Then the rivers did the work and not Hercules at all. I thank them heartily. I'll pay them a tribute of wine this afternoon. And I'll thank you, Phyleus, to keep to your washing and to speak when I permit it. Sons are a father's bane, Hercules. You did well to kill all yours when they were small enough.'

The young man blushed with outraged embarrassment. 'Father! May the gods punish you for saying such things. Pay your debts. If you promised Hercules anything pay

55

it to him now. He *has* cleaned the stables. Truly he has!'

For all his idleness, Augeas could move quickly inside his rags. He launched a kick and a push at his son that toppled the boy off the hilltop and rolled him down through thistles and thorns. 'Run away and starve. I've done with you and your treachery. I disinherit you,' and he bared his yellow teeth.

Phyleus tried to get to his feet. 'Disinherit me? Of what, father? This pigsty of a kingdom? A million flies waiting in attendance? You can keep it!'

Augeas drew a sword so rusty and encrusted that it looked like a stalactite wrenched off the ceiling of a cave. The cutting edge was blunt when he jabbed it into Hercules, but when he hurled it at his son, Phyleus fell, clutching his head. Hercules looked down at the graze on his chest and fingered the blood thoughtfully. Then he picked up King Augeas like something objectionable he had found in a mousetrap, and throwing him across the back of a goat, sent the animal scampering and skipping out of the valley and out of the kingdom.

'I regret, my lord, that you will have to wear the crown, now that your father has gone,' he told Phyleus. And he left the lad fervently washing his hair in the river so that his head should be deserving of a coronation.

8

Birds and Beasts

Eurystheus woke up with that accustomed quake of his heart and the usual question in his head: what impossible task could he find next for Hercules? Then he remembered the Augean Stables. That task would take tens of years, if indeed Hercules ever accomplished it. And the king lay back and wallowed in the thought of dung, more dung, and yet more dung. For several years he would be able to sleep in peace.

'Hercules is in the vestibule, my lord,' said the slave who came to wake him. 'Should I let him into the throne-room or do you wish to enter your chest first?'

Eurystheus gave a convulsive shudder, and he snatched the covers up over his head. 'Who? Where? Send him away. Lock him up! Offer up prayers!' Slowly, however, the king emerged again, white-faced but grinning. 'He's failed. The Augean Stables defeated him. I can sink him in a dungeon. He'll beg me to forgive him, but I won't! I'll send him back there to go on mucking out! You'll see! That's the way of it.'

The slave crept uncertainly out of the room, but stopped to listen by the door as the king's excitable voice started up again. 'You'll see! He's failed. He couldn't do it. You'll see!'

And a female voice replied, 'I think not, Eurystheus. You must try harder. Such a simple task I gave you, and you make so much of it . . . '

The servant peeped round the curtain that hung across the doorway. But he could see no one: only the king struggling into his robes like a man smothered by a collapsing tent.

Somewhere between the bedchamber and the throne-room, Eurystheus learned how Augeas had been turned out of his kingdom on the back of a goat and how Phyleus had been made king in his father's place. The idea so outraged Eurystheus that he forgot his fear, forgot his bronze hidey-hole and burst into the throne-room shaking his fists with fury. 'Is this how you serve a master? Is this how you humble yourself to the will of the gods? What gives you the right to be a kingmaker?'

He was confronted by the sight of an excitable crowd of women, their backs turned on him and their faces towards Hercules who sat on the steps of the throne listening to them. They did not even notice Eurystheus.

'Huge they are—wings as wide as this!'

' . . . with legs like cranes, and beaks . . . '

' . . . oh, beaks as sharp as cuttle and claws that rip . . . '

' . . . They steal the sheep!'

' . . . They strip the trees!'

' . . . *They eat our children*, Hercules!'

Hercules nodded sadly. 'I've heard of such birds. But what do you want the king to do? Send an army?'

'No! How can anyone fight an enemy in the sky? An army would be torn to pieces!'

' . . . No, we want to come here, Hercules . . . '

' . . . We need somewhere to live! The birds have torn

the roofs off our houses to steal us out of our beds! Ask him for us. Put our case to the . . . '

One by one, the people in the room caught sight of the king and fell to their knees. He looked them up and down, eyes bulging and cheeks puffed up with rage. 'Well? What have you to say to me, Hercules of Thebes?'

Hercules went and knelt, in all humility, at the king's feet, and pressed his forehead to Eurystheus's thigh. 'I humbly beg a favour on behalf of these people, your subjects from the region of Stamphylia.'

Eurystheus snatched his robe away as if it were on fire, and shrieked, in little staccato bursts, 'No! No! They *can't* come and live here. They *can't* live anywhere except where they belong. I forbid it. They can all go back where they came from. And you'll go with them to deal with these *birds*. If they eat you—well, that's the will of the gods . . . And good riddance!'

Turning his bowed head, Hercules caught the eye of a Stamphylian woman and winked. 'I humbly thank my master for your graciousness. You grant my favour without me even having to speak it.' And he hurried out of the room, ushering the women ahead of him like a brood of chickens. The taste of triumph in the king's mouth turned so sour that he spat.

The mucous fish of the sea softly slip out of the hand. The beasts of the land are wrapped in fur or hide, and the birds of the air are commonly the softest of all, carrying flakes of the sky beneath their downy feathers. But the bladebills of Stamphylia are not soft. There is no tender frailness in their skin-webbed wings. The brittle skeleton is razor-sharp and the bones barely cushioned by flesh. A bladebill flies like a rattle of thrown sticks, and its claws sink deep into its prey. At the touch of yielding meat, its head begins to saw and its beak to slash and its claws to close in an ecstasy of greed, and it shreds and tears and scatters; and a tongue as long and thin as an eel flickers about for the blood. A cow staggers under its weight; a straw roof buckles, and a man can do nothing but sink to his knees and die.

When Hercules arrived in Stamphylia with the babble of women, they were met by the sight of towns torn down, markets stripped bare, vines trampled into the purple ground, and villages in ruins. Slashed black trees wept sap through their wounded bark. The bladebills were mustered in the topmost branches of the black trees, stepping from foot to foot, groping the air with their claws and peering across the bare countryside.

At the sight of fresh meat coming, they took off, three, four, five at a time, and covered the sky. Like hide tents blowing across a desert they flapped slowly, noisily, piercing their own flapping with occasional blood-curdling shrieks. When their 'food' found shelter in a cave, they scratched vilely on the stone cliff outside and jabbed their beaks in at the door for a while before rattling back into the sky.

The cave was already crowded with people chased there by the bladebills. They looked up now, with hollow cheeks and haunted eyes, and covered their ears against the sound of the bladebills flying. The only food they had salvaged—sacks of flour—was mildewy with damp, and a greedy fire in the centre of the floor licked up whatever wisps of fuel they fed it. To the people in the cave, Hercules was just another empty mouth, and he looked like a man with a big appetite. They were not glad to see him.

Their fears were confirmed when he said, 'Make dough! Make bread dough out of all the flour you've got.'

'Do as he says,' urged the women who had fetched

him. 'He killed the Hydra! He caught the Erymanthian Boar! Do what he tells you!'

Water was scarce. They had to wait for it to drip-drip off the roof into the bowls of flour: it was two days before the flour was a solid mass. 'There's no oven to bake it,' protested the Stamphylians, 'and look at the mould—it's not fit to eat!'

'All the better,' said Hercules, dragging the dough towards the mouth of the cave, tub after tub after tub.

The bladebills ambushed him whenever he stepped outside. They swooped and tore at him. But the Nemean Lion's skin defied their talons, and the sword of Hermes lopped off their trailing legs. Like craneflies on a summer night, more and more came rattling out of the sky. Hercules fended them off with Apollo's arrows so they soon turned to eating the dough instead.

Some plunged in their beaks and could not pull them out again. Some tore off lumps and swallowed them. The dough stuck in their gullets, or weighed them down, until their wings could not lift them. In some, the mildew poisoned them like lead in a swan; it turned their grey throats green and their brains an unruly purple, and they thrashed about, wounding the other birds.

Once blood was drawn, the birds overhead folded their wings and dived out of the sky as cormorants plunge on fish in the sea. They did not fall on the dough or on to Hercules's sword but on to their fellow birds. And while they gouged and fought and intertangled their spiny wings, Hercules waded in amongst them, and notched the blade of Hermes's sword on their sharp bones, their wire-sharp sinews.

Just once, he felt a plume of feathers brush his cheek and, when he looked up, thought he saw a sandalled heel treading the air near his head. But then his vision was filled by a skin-webbed wing as big as a sail, and a

61

spread claw snatched at his face. Afterwards, nobody watching from the mouth of the cave mentioned seeing a god at Hercules's side.

They bathed his cuts and groomed his lionskin and disentangled the claws of bladebills from his hair. They turned their eyes away from the carnage around the baskets of dough . . . and they said nothing, not a word—as if the air was better empty, even of words. Not a sheep bleated; not a cow lowed: there were no sheep or cows. There were no chickens either, nor horses, nor goats nor songbirds nor geese. There was not even the rustle of grain filling the fields. Stamphylia was stripped bare. The bladebills had eaten it all.

'You only had to wait,' said Hercules when they tried to offer him payment in bits and pieces of gold. 'I did nothing. The birds would have turned on each other for food sooner or later. Destroyers always destroy themselves. Do you know the kingdom of Elis? No, don't shudder like that. Augeas has gone now, and the stables don't smell. If you send your shepherds to his son, Phyleus, and tell him you've come for Hercules's share of the animals, he will give you half of all the goats and horses and cows in the Augean stables. They should help to re-stock Stamphylia.'

Then a clamour of cheering and clapping and laughter burst from the people and rose up over Hercules's head. It followed him all the way to the borders of Stamphylia, like a flock of seagulls following a ship.

Poseidon the Earth-Shaker, the Earthquake-Maker, the god of the oceans, sat in the blue shallows of the sea and watched a flock of seagulls fly over. From beneath the sea's surface, they looked like small white fish swimming, but even through the filtering foam their raucous voices were audible. It seemed to Poseidon that they were shouting, 'H-erk-culee! H-erk-culeee! H-erk-culee!'

The world was noisy with talk of Zeus's mortal son. The sea, flaking gossip off the shores of the world, washed it in at Poseidon's ears; it filtered down to him like water-shrimp. Soon even the sea god's kingdom would be awash with news of Hercules's feats of strength and heroics.

On Olympus, Hera slammed the doors of heaven while lesser gods conspired on the staircases. Zeus, thinking he was unobserved, and resting his head nonchalantly on one hand, took sidelong glances down at the sea-encircling world in the hope of catching sight of his son. Once, when he saw Hercules overrun and outnumbered by a flock of vile birds, he had whispered in Hermes's ear, 'Help him! Go on!' and Hermes had flown to the rescue. But then Zeus had wrapped himself in cloud and fingered his beard and sworn that matters were out of his hands. Hercules must suffer the fate allotted to him.

'Hercules is a common murderer,' Hera would snarl imperiously. But when she was gone, the gods would scamper to the parapets of heaven and watch the continuing Labours of Hercules. 'Twelve years!' they would whisper. 'If he survives for twelve years, he's no ordinary mortal.'

And hearing this, Zeus banged the arms of his throne and whispered to himself, 'If he survives for twelve years he shall be one of the Immortals. By my head, he shall!'

All this was known to Poseidon, the sea god, although the news had to drift to him on the tide. For no one thought to visit his oceanic realm while there were the Labours of Hercules to distract them. 'They'll be calling him a god soon and building temples to him, you mark what I say!' But there was no one there to mark him. Every ship that sailed overhead was filled with sailors talking about Hercules. Every giggle of naked girls that bathed in the surf was sighing for a sight of Hercules. The sea grew muddy with Poseidon's vexation.

Only King Minos, monarch of Crete, was too busy making daily sacrifice at the sea god's temple to take an interest in the stories of Hercules. Poseidon had great hopes of King Minos.

'I'll give them all something more worthy to speak of than *Hercules*,' muttered Poseidon. And he made, out of the shining hide of the ocean, a bull. He stuffed it with krill and gave it hooves of coral. Its eyes were Elmo's Fire and its horns were the shed tusks of the narwhal. It stood twenty hands high and was as placid as a summer sea. 'Minos shall sacrifice this blue beast to me, the Bull-Maker, the Earthquake-Maker, the Sea-Shifter . . . and the whole world will cast its eyes over the sacrifice and remember to fear Poseidon!'

The Cretans found Poseidon's blue bull wandering on the sea shore. People ran down to the beach and up to the palace. 'Lord king! Lord king! The gods have sent you such a bull!'

And when Minos saw it he ordered garlands to be made for its neck and said, 'Such a bull! By the gods, such an animal! Poseidon sent it. Yes, that's the truth of it. The great sea god desires a fitting sacrifice. A whole herd of prime bullocks wouldn't make as fit a sacrifice as this. Sound the horns! Summon the people! Offer up the beast on the altar of Poseidon! I shall make the cut myself!'

Heralds whose brass horns coiled around them like rampant pythons blew the summons. And from every small mountain sheepfold, every fishing village on the southern shore, every cattle farm, the people of Crete set off to see the king's latest devout sacrifice.

'No, wait,' said Minos to his High Priest. 'I want to

64

look at it for a while longer. See how it steps! See how it brandishes its horns!'

'But the people have been summoned, lord king . . . '

'Then sacrifice a dozen bullocks out of my own corral. Tomorrow the blue bull. Tell them tomorrow. I just want to look at it for a while longer.'

And as he looked, Minos began to question whether Poseidon had indeed sent the bull. 'Perhaps one of the other gods sent it. What a blasphemy it would be to sacrifice it on the wrong altar! . . . Or perhaps it was a present. Perhaps Poseidon was *giving* it to me in return for all my sacrifices. Perhaps he wants me to breed from it. Perhaps . . . ' And the more he speculated, the less he wanted to cut the throat of the blue bull. 'Perhaps it just wandered up out of the sea. Perhaps Poseidon doesn't even know it's here. Perhaps if he saw it, he'd want it for his own herd. And what would he do to me if I'd made the mistake of cutting its throat. Perhaps I ought to keep it by, until the facts are more plain. Perhaps . . . perhaps if I build a corral with high enough walls, Poseidon won't even hear tell of the beast and I can keep it . . . Oh!' Minos clapped his hand over his mouth to stop himself speaking any more blasphemy out loud. But in the secrecy of his head, he went on thinking it. He was now absolutely determined that the blue bull should not be spilt on the altar of the sea god. He would keep the animal hidden away where he could gaze at its beauty day and night.

The High Priest came and said, 'The people are still assembled at the Temple, lord king. Will you set an hour for the sacrifice of the blue bull?'

'Blue bull?' said Minos. 'What blue bull? What are you talking about? Send them home. No more sacrifices today. Blue bull? Don't know what the man is babbling about. What blue bull?'

*　*　*

'WHAT BLUE BULL?' cried Poseidon, and the veins in his forehead made channels of a different blue in the seething ocean. 'WHAT BLUE BULL?' And he scrabbled together the phosphorescence of a tropical night and hurled it at Crete. '*That* blue bull, you blasphemous dog!'

Encamped around the Temple of Poseidon, the people of Crete were disappointed. They had seen the blue bull being led up from the beach and wanted another glimpse of its glossy blue hide and the sweep of its ivory horns and the glow of its eyes.

They were starting to settle down in the sand for a night's sleep when they saw, all of a sudden, their own shadows cast black as daytime, and a comet of incandescent light burst over the western horizon. A faggot of phosphorescence spun slowly over their heads as though the air was syrup-thick. Poseidon had hurled a thunderbolt. But at what? At whom? The people leapt to their feet and stared. For there, between palace and beach, stood the blue bull.

The knot of light hit it on the side of the head, bursting on its serrated horn and splashing like mercury into its eyes and nostrils. Its mouth dripped phosphorescence. Its hide shuddered. Its wits shattered. Sweat dripped from its hide like rain.

At first, the people on the beach were transfixed by the beauty of the beast shrouded in dripping light. Even when it began to paw the ground and bellow, they did not think to run. Only when it came ploughing down the beach, its horns rooting up gouts of sand to right and left, did they run for the sea, run for the dunes, run for the boats. The blue bull smashed the boats and sank them. It smashed all the fishermen's shacks and the beach groynes. It turned back to the palace and crazed the ceramic walls with its iron skull. It maddened itself in ropes of clematis and vine torn down off the trellises. It threw the carts in the palace yard over the sea wall, and gouged its letterless name in the great oak doors.

Buttresses fell away. Plaster was flayed off like skin, and left the timbers of the building exposed. High up on the roof, King Minos howled his terror. 'Kill it! Kill it! Someone kill the beast!' His army ignored his commands and cowered alongside him with their arms over their heads.

'What must I do? *What must I do?'* yelled Minos at the oil-black sea.

But Poseidon had no advice to offer. Smug in his revenge, he turned his back on Crete and strode towards his dark deep-sea caverns.

So the people answered Minos instead. They called back up at the roof of the palace, *'Send for Hercules! Send for Hercules!'*

Poseidon stopped in his tracks and put his hands over his ears: 'That name again!'

On the roof, Minos said, 'Who? What did they say? Send for him! I don't know who he is. I've never heard of him. But send for Hercules!'

Poseidon curled his lip. 'Very good. Let them send for him. My blue bull can split him and spill him on my altar for a sacrifice. Then we'll hear the last of Hercules!'

9

Poseidon's Pride and Joy

The prayers of King Minos and the people of Crete hung over the island like a haze of heat. And the murmurings of Poseidon reached Hera, too, where she sat on the parapets of heaven, sulking.

So it was not long before the queen of the gods was slipping ghostlike to Eurystheus's bedside to whisper in his ear: 'Send Hercules to tame the mad blue bull!'

Hercules listened to the king's command and nodded. His face had taken on a strange illegibility, like the carvings of a lost civilization, half overgrown with creepers. A wild tangle of beard obscured his mouth. Eurystheus thought there was something very bull-like in the figure crouched in front of his brass trunk, and though the streets outside his palace were lined with citizens of Thebes grizzling and tearing their clothes in sorrow at the dangers facing Hercules, Eurystheus feared more for Poseidon's bull.

The roads of Crete were lined with people, too— caravans of carts and wagons moved families, households, whole villages from one end of the island to the other in an effort to escape the blue bull. But though the beast returned often to the rubble of the king's palace to throw down another statue and buckle yet more pillars, its frenzy would take it from the north coast to the south, from the east to the west. Over the mountains and through the olive groves it raged, with a hunger for devastation that was never filled. As the rocks of the sea are festooned with the wreckage of ships, so its horns dangled ropes, garlands, and torn cloth. Its hide was stained morocco red with blood, and flies followed behind it like the scavengers who follow an army to pick over the battlefields. People knew when it was coming, not only by the trembling of the ground and the cloud of dirty dust but by the canopy of vultures that circled over its spoil. In their terror, the people of Crete came to believe that the bull was not mad at all, for it destroyed with such a terrible methodical efficiency. Not an acre of island dry-land had been spared by its pounding hooves.

But inside the bull's head were far worse scenes of devastation. Not a thought remained that was not splashed with burning phosphorescence. Not a view came into his eyeball but it was struck through with fork lightning. The night seemed as bright and shadeless as noon. The world burned round him like an incandescent cage. So even when exhaustion griped at him he went on and on destroying.

So when he saw a bearded, thick-set figure ride into the royal harbour on the prow of a fast-moving ship, the blue bull was filled with the need to destroy both man and ship. His crescent slash of horns burst the ship to fragments, and the mast fell groaning and impaled the sea. But when the bull shook off the spars and sheets of the shattered ship, he saw that the man was ashore now and stood, arms folded, on the quayside. A great roar of voices echoed in the bull's ears: 'Hercules! Hercules!'—a thunderous migraine of noise that made the beast roll its head on its neck.

Still Hercules did not move.

'Fight it, Hercules! Kill it! Cut it to pieces!' bawled the fishermen cowering among the ruins of the sea wall. 'You killed the Hydra didn't you?'

But Hercules did not move.

'Sacrifice it to the sea god! Cut its throat on Poseidon's altar,' King Minos called feebly from the broken parapets above the beach. But Hercules did not move.

The blue bull pawed the ground, lowered its head, grated the tip of one horn on the stone quay. But not until its flank twitched and hurled it forwards did Hercules turn on his heel and run. He ran and the bull ran after him. He dodged between the rubble and splintered bollards, but the bull cannoned through all obstacles and gained on him quickly. On the sand, both feet and hooves sank in. But on the marble steps of the promenade the beast's hooves skidded, and Hercules saved himself from the slash of the horns. Through the main street, through the ruins of the pounded palace, through its flowery yards and sweet-smelling places, Hercules fled the bull.

'Shame on you for a coward, Hercules!' shouted the cowering crowds. 'Stop and fight!'

But Hercules went on running. He ran the bull up hills until its blue lungs heaved. He ran it down hills till its hind quarters quaked, and he ran it through coppices of tightly packed trees. He ran it through briars till its flanks bled blue brine. He ran it over bare white rocks in the heat of the day, till its withers steamed salt sweat. And last of all he ran into the sea, and the blue bull followed him, bellowing through its upturned nostrils, its legs continuing to run even when it could no longer touch bottom.

From inside its head, the blue bull looked up at the

agonizing brightness of the sky and the cutting edge of the spinning sun. Waves broke into his breathing passages; waves broke into his eyes. The great weight of horn on his head dragged like the ice on a masthead that overturns an arctic ship. From somewhere overhead came the sound of rasping breaths, and as the bull's blue face sank beneath the surface, he realized that the rasping noise was his own breath and that he was drowning.

Hercules swam on, even though each arm felt like lead as he lifted it out of the water. He swam until he heard a bellow behind him suddenly cut short by a gurgling gulp. Looking over his shoulder, he saw the blue bull sink. The phosphorescence of its eyes glowed through the water: as he swam back, he could see its great bulk drifting immobile between surface and sea bed.

Diving down, he groped for the great sweep of horn, and drove back up towards the surface: climbing through the water felt like climbing a rungless ladder. But at last he broke surface among the floating debris of garlands, ropes, and cloth that had washed off the bull. He set off for the shore, swimming on his back, and beached the bull on the gentle slope of a sandy bay.

Side by side they lay, the hot sun steaming out of them every last desire to move. The bull stopped snorting and choking, and breathed in big, noisy sighs. Hercules tugged gently at its flicking ears and combed vinestalks and seaweed out of its blue hide with his fingers. For several hours the bull lay slumped in the warm sand, sunbathing. Hercules was wondering how to get it to its feet again when a groan (such as a volcano gives before it erupts) sent a veil of sand shimmering down all the dunes. A man waded down towards Hercules through the hot sand.

He was a tree-like man. The bones of his shins splayed into his shambling feet like trunk into roots. His green hair spread out like a leaf-canopy over his head, shoulders, and back. His mouth was big enough to harbour a barn owl and all its chicks.

'So you're Hercules. To think a brat so small could grieve my father so sore,' he said, grinding the words to pieces between his teeth. 'I am Antaeus, son of Poseidon, and you are an offence in his eyes!'

'I am? An offence to Poseidon. The gods forbid it!' Hercules went towards Antaeus, his arms outstretched in apology. 'I'm sure I never meant it. Have I failed to make sacrifice? Have I missed a festival? I've been so busy, you see.'

Antaeus took hold of his arm, wrist, and elbow, and thrashed Hercules bodily against the ground. The blue bull scrambled to its feet, bellowing resentfully, but Antaeus picked it up and threw it into the shallows, where it wallowed, winded. Thinking that the element of surprise had been his downfall, Hercules got up, adopted the stance of a wrestler and said, 'Come on, then: the Erymanthean Boar was bigger than you!' The next he knew, the sky was wheeling past, full of little lights like fireflies; Antaeus was shaking Hercules like a rug.

Sprawled on the ground, his head in a bush, Hercules found himself looking at the great sinewy tendons of the giant's calf and knee, as once again Antaeus dealt with the charging bull: one-handed he up-ended it and bowled it back down the beach. With the exertion of the throw, each knotty varicose blood-vessel pumped and the veins in his braced legs swelled green, as if succour from the ground were rising up through his legs like sap through a tree. The feet were entrenched deeply in the sand, and over a large area round about the sea-pinks and couch-grasses were withering away. The magma of the earth and the vigour of every spring was feeding the giant with energy.

Hercules was still lying prostrate on the ground when Antaeus finished with the bull. He grinned at the sight of Hercules's ashen face, and came scuffing across the dune at a loping run. So inviting was the prospect of crushing Hercules, gut and bone, that he could not resist leaping in the air to stamp down with both feet on the vulnerable spine.

But Hercules met him in mid-air, curving his back and bending his shoulders to intercept Antaeus and carry him, at a run, along the shore. The giant slapped and champed at him, until Hercules thought his ears must have been torn off and all his hair rooted up. But, above his head, the raging voice rose to a higher and higher pitch and the jabbing of knees in his back grew less and less painful. Antaeus reached and strained to put down one finger or scrape one sandal along the ground. But Hercules only held him higher and higher—at arm's length finally. Poseidon's son grew limper and limper, like a dying tree branch.

'Stop!'

The sea gave a convulsive heave, and waves about to break on the shore arched their backs with dismay. Poseidon the Sea-Breaker, the Earthquake-Maker, came wading through the surf like a shepherd stumbling through a flock of sheep. 'Stop it, Hercules! Or by all the rents and tears I've made in the ocean bed, I'll wash Crete off the face of the sea. That's my son you're holding!'

Hercules took a deep breath and closed his eyes. He could feel the clammy presence of the sea god, like a wet sea-fret against his face. 'I know it, Lord Poseidon. I do know it's your son. And if I once put him down, he'll tear me to pieces: I know that, too.'

Poseidon ground his teeth. 'I see it now. I see the likeness. I see why they talk about you as if your throne were already carved on Olympus!'

Like an uprooted plant, Antaeus was wilting fast. He called out whimperingly to his father who hissed with exasperation: 'What price, then, Hercules? I'll give you one of my own sea-horses if you'll set him down!'

'Oh. Thank you,' said Hercules, genuinely and pleasantly surprised. 'I've always wanted a horse. But all I want is a promise. If I put him down, he won't tear me to pieces.'

'By your father's name, I swear it,' said Poseidon.

Hercules was so struck by the oath that he put down Antaeus almost absent-mindedly. Fingers and feet scraped feebly at the ground, then dug in deeply. The hairs on the nape of Antaeus's neck curled, and the sear autumnal yellow of his back throbbed green again. He seemed to swell, as buds and catkins swell. When he grappled Hercules to the ground, it was with all the strength of the jungle that tears down cities with its inexorable creepers. Antaeus bared his teeth to bite Hercules's throat across.

'Antaeus! Leave him! Come away!' snapped Poseidon. 'Would you make a liar of your own father? Look at you. You're a disgrace to me. Didn't you hear my words . . . ?' And mighty Poseidon, the Earth-Shaper, the Earthquake-Maker frogmarched his son, mumbling and muttering, all the way along the beach until they were out of sight.

The blue bull had gone, too. In the place where Hercules had last seen it stood a palomino horse, as golden as the sand and with a mane very like the surf. Even far away from the bright, reflective flicker of the sea that mane kept its strangely blue tinge.

Because nobody expected Hercules to be riding a horse, he was through the city gates and had dismounted in the palace yard before any message could be got to Eurystheus.

So the king was surprised while taking dinner with his children.

Hercules was surprised, too, because he had not realized that Eurystheus had children. He was covered in confusion, for fear his wild appearance might frighten the girls.

But though Eurystheus dived under the table as quick as a rabbit, the princesses of Argos lolled unperturbed on their couches and lobbed apple cores at Hercules. 'What are you doing down there, father?'

'I . . . er . . . dropped some . . . er . . . bread.' Eurystheus emerged in some confusion. 'Blue bull tamed, is it, bond-slave?'

'Tamed, cousin, yes.'

'Cousin? Is that what he calls you, father? Is he allowed to call you _cousin_?' said the oldest girl shrilly. 'You're too soft with the slaves.' She looked out of the window. 'Oh, what a horse! What a beautiful horse! I want it. Is it yours, slave? Slaves don't have horses. I want it.'

'It was a gift from the great sea god Poseidon, mistress,' said Hercules, expressionless behind his beard. 'It was given to me for sparing Antaeus, the Earth-Shaker's . . . '

'I want a horse,' said the child.

Eurystheus, who was hurrying from wall to wall of the room examining maps and lists, wagged his head from side to side impatiently. 'Give Admeta the horse, Hercules. It's hers. I confiscate it. Why are you back so soon? I haven't thought of . . . '

'Don't want _that_ horse,' said Admeta piercingly.

'What kind of horse do you want, mistress?' Hercules was quick to ask since he was extremely loath to part with Poseidon's present.

The child bared her teeth at him in a travesty of a

grin, and stuck out her tongue. 'Want one of King Diomedes's horses.'

'I'll get you one,' said Hercules in a flash.

'All of them. I want all of them. They're such jolly creatures.'

'I'll get all of them,' said Hercules with a glance over his shoulder. His glance met Eurystheus's as the king cast a look of delight towards his daughter.

'Yes, yes. Get the horses. Diomedes is a barbarian. I never liked the man.'

Hastily Hercules left the room, rejoicing in having kept his beautiful horse.

'Is that the man who keeps you so busy, father? Is that the one you call "that damned Hercules"?'

'That's him, my darling girl. The gods placed a heavy burden on me when they put Hercules in my charge. Finding ways of keeping him busy—finding work that's a fitting punishment for a murderer.'

'Oh, don't you worry about that, father. I can think of *plenty* of tasks for him to do. I can think of lots of terrible torments.'

Her father beamed at her indulgently and settled to his meal again, pausing between courses to pat Admeta on the head. 'Tell me, my darling girl,' he said, 'I've heard about that barbarian Diomedes. But what's so jolly about these horses of his?'

Admeta shrugged and replied through a big mouthful of food, 'Well, they *eat* people, don't they?'

10

Queen of the Amazons

King Diomedes was fond of his horses. Or rather he found them useful. For he murdered and executed so many people that without his stable of hungry horses, the litter of dead bodies would have piled up. Diomedes's realm was spotless. His horses were fat and sleek.

So he objected to the idea of giving up his horses to the Princess Admeta. In fact he told Hercules in no uncertain terms, his sword half out of its scabbard, that he would feed him, live and kicking, to the horses and watch while they ate him. So Hercules accompanied Diomedes as far as the stables before picking him up, sword and all, and throwing him over the door.

First the horses ate Diomedes, then they ate his sword, and all that was left of the king of Thrace was a space in the market square after his subjects happily tore down his statue.

Admeta grew bored with her new pets when she was forbidden to feed them on the palace servants. Eurystheus took one look at their long, gnashing teeth, their malevolent yellow eyes, and shut himself in his brass box with the doors of the palace barred. He told Hercules to drive them to Arcadia and release them there, where the sun god's own horses grazed.

'If he takes them I shall want another present,' said Princess Admeta whiningly.

Eurystheus gnawed his lip. His daughter knew how to bully her father. 'Did you have something in mind, my darling girl?'

'Yes,' she snapped. She was not unlike one of the Thracian horses when her teeth were bared. 'I want . . . I want . . . I want the jewelled belt of the Amazon queen!'

The servant below the throne gave a low whistle, cut short by a blow from the king. Admeta's younger sisters gazed at her in admiration: they could think of nothing so desirable as the jewelled belt of the Amazon queen.

'I wouldn't want a war,' mumbled Eurystheus. 'They're very ferocious women, those Amazons. They're not as gentle and ladylike as you, my darling Admeta. I mean, they'll kill a man just for *being* a man. I mean . . . '

'You mean I can't have it,' said Admeta, nipping off the words with her sharp little teeth.

'Of course . . . if Hercules could fetch it without starting a war . . . '

Hercules's face behind its beard expressed nothing, nothing at all.

'I don't care how he does it, but *I want that belt*!' Something in the tone of Admeta's voice made a little shiver run down the king's spine: it was so much like that nagging little voice that scuttled from cranny to nook of his bedchamber and lurked at the foot of his bed when there was no one there to be seen.

'In the name of Hera—*go and get that belt*!' he stormed

at Hercules, darting towards him. But he ran away again, back to his throne, as Hercules got wearily to his feet.

Hippolyta, queen of the Amazons, was as black as oil—as black as the night sea that seethes unseen on to beaches of black sand. She was tall—taller than a totem mouthing magic under a jungle moon. She moved with the slithering, sliding pride of a black panther. Her eyes were dark—dark like the sun's eclipse at noon or the moon's eclipse at midnight. The smell of her oiled and corded hair was strange as the scent of the black orchid. And round her hips, like the cable of a treasure ship, hung a belt of intricate gold thread. Plaited and whorled and fastened by two clasped golden hands, its strands, like water twisting and turning through rapids, parted to right and left of precious gems then splashed in golden tassels to below her bare knees.

The commanders of defeated armies claimed that the belt of Hippolyta had magic powers, that it could dazzle whole divisions of men. But then war-worn male soldiers defeated by a band of mere *women* tend to make excuses.

Hercules did not make the mistake of underestimating the Amazons. He had heard the rumours of their warrior prowess, and he believed every word. He walked into the Amazon camp without a sword or spear or shield, his hands high above his head in surrender.

Out from their woven huts, out from behind trees, out of heaps of corn husks where they had been sleeping, Amazonian women uncurled like blackest cats. They took up their long, oval shields and short throwing-spears and beat spear on shield in a slow drumming that speeded up to a frenzied clatter. Their prisoners—the men they had set to mending baskets, washing clothes, and sweeping out the huts—crept away with their hands over their ears.

Closer and closer the circle of women moved, jabbing their weapons towards his face and stamping the ground in time with the drumming. The harsh, high shriek of their voices pecked at him. 'What are you?' 'Who sent you?' 'We'll find a use for you!' 'How small he is.' 'What a puny specimen.' 'Too weak to carry a sword, even.' 'What a cowardly weakling.' 'Speak. Admit that you're a worthless man too scared to carry weapons.'

'I am neither man nor woman,' said Hercules. 'I am a story-teller. I came to tell a story to the queen of the Amazons whose name is . . . '

'I know my name,' said a deep, reverberating voice. 'I do not like it to be held in the mouth of a mere man.' The crowd of women parted and there stood Hippolyta, taller than any there and more beautiful than the black-limbed ebon trees. 'Did I send for a story-teller? Did I ask you to come? What do I want with stories?'

'Then I shall leave and take my story with me, for I have no trade where I have no audience. I just thought it would interest you, since it concerns kings and queens and the gods themselves. But no matter . . . Good-day, lady.'

'Wait! Wait a moment.'

An untold story is like a locked chest without a key. It tantalizes. It tempts. From the icy lands of snow and whale to the sweating jungle shade, it is valued the world over.

'Maybe I've heard it,' said Hippolyta sceptically.

'Kill me if you have,' said Hercules. And a few moments later he was seated on a rug of zebra skin while Hippolyta reclined on a couch of spotted hide in the privacy of her cool, dark hut.

Hercules began to tell his own life story, and while Hippolyta listened, her warrior women sulked outside, swatting at tedious flies with their large, listless hands.

In the gaping holes between the tree-tops, the moisture from the humid leaves dripped like saliva, and the sweltering sun made a steamy rainbow that intertwined with the creepers and dangling vines. Down this rainbow came Hera, queen of the gods, her black hair close-cloaking her sallow body. She came down, hand-over-hand, so slowly, so silently that the dozing women thought they were dreaming her . . .

'So the worthless man was enslaved to this small and spiteful king as a punishment, and sent here and there across the face of the wide Earth to kill monsters and capture great prizes and do unpleasant tasks. He had no part in deciding the tasks, no right to refuse them. No profit or joy came to him by his Labours. To fail or refuse would be death. So he killed the Hydra, he cleaned the Augean stables, and he captured the golden stag of Cerynia. All might have gone well but for his last, most fearful and most wicked task. He was ordered to fetch—imagine it!—the belt of the queen of the Amazons for the king's spoilt daughter!'

He shot a glance at Hippolyta. Her hands moved involuntarily to her belt, then she raised herself along the couch like a lion about to spring. She reached for her throwing spear and lifted it over one shoulder. Then the purple shadows of her black face scattered in a laugh. 'Hercules! What gall! What a bare-faced, shameless trickster you are!' she cried, tossing her corded hair far down her back. 'But you lied to me.'

'Not a word, lady, on my life!'

'Oh yes you did. Don't deny it. You said that you were

unremarkable and you are nothing of the kind!' and she made a cat-like leap on to the zebra rug beside him. 'You're extraordinary. Quite outstanding, for a man.'

'Then you'll give me the belt?'

'I do believe I will—and afterwards I'll come and take it back and teach that spiteful little king not to make a plaything for his children out of a brave and noble story-teller!' She began to unclasp the belt.

Hera whispered softer than the sound of the caterpillars dropping through the trees, pressing her lips against the delicate ears of the warrior women. 'Stir yourselves! Since when did you let a MAN creep in to the royal hut of your beloved queen? Think! Ask yourself! What weapons did he have hidden beneath that lionskin? What poisons are smeared on those hairy arms? With his bare hands he murdered his wife and all his little daughters. And I tell you, Hercules has come here to murder your queen and steal her golden belt! What will become of the Amazons when their queen is dead? Will you let squat Hercules make you his slaves and dancing girls. Quick! Quick! Kill him quickly or Hippolyta is lost!'

Just as Hippolyta was about to lay the jewelled belt in Hercules's hands, the fibrous walls of the hut were ripped to shreds by axes and jabbing spears. The warrior women came through the walls, came through the reeded roof, crammed the sunny doorway, hooting and shrieking their bloodcurdling war-cries.

One leapt directly on to Hercules. All he could do to defend himself was to wrap both arms round her so that her hands were pinned to her sides and her body shielded him against the thrusting spears. The women hesitated rather than plunge their weapons through the woman's body. Seeing how his armful of Amazon protected him,

Hercules backed through the door. Then slinging the warrior across his back, he ran. He did not stop running until the shrieking of the deep-jungle parrots all around drowned out the shrieks from behind him.

'What's your name?' he said as he ran.

'I'll die before I tell you that!' The woman's voice came jolting out of her.

'What's your name? Do tell me.'

'Never! Now put me down,' and she bit into him.

'Ow! Stop that! Why did you all attack me back there? I meant no harm, I swear it!'

'No harm? Ha! You're a filthy assassin and a thief!'

'Says who?'

'Says . . . says . . . I don't know who says it . . . The Amazons say it. I, General Menalippe, say it.'

Suddenly, out of a tree, directly in his path, a long sinuous figure dropped down. It was Hippolyta who had outrun her women, outrun Hercules, outrun her good nature. 'My women say you were planning to kill me.'

'That's a lie.'

'Women don't lie. Men lie,' hissed Hippolyta.

Hercules stood General Menalippe down in front of him as a shield, one arm round her body, one arm round her throat.

'That's a dirty trick,' said Hippolyta. 'How typical of a man!'

'You mean women aren't afraid to die?'

'Absolutely not! We scorn death!'

The general wriggled in Hercules's arms, but he had tight hold of her. Hippolyta's jabbing spear could not pierce Hercules without killing Menalippe. He could feel the hostage trembling from head to foot. 'Do you scorn death, Menalippe?' he said in her ear.

'Let me go!' she sobbed.

83

'What is the life of an Amazon worth, madam?' he asked the queen.

'More than the life of a man.'

'More than a tin belt, then. That's all I ask. Give it to me and I'll let her go.'

Queen Hippolyta slowly unclasped the belt one-handed, the other hand still brandishing her spear. She lashed at him with the golden tassels and they wrapped around his arm and hand.

'You are deceived in me, madam. I never meant you harm. The story I told you was true. I hope one day you will believe me. Now, I shall take General Menalippe here with me and set her free when I reach the sea-shore safely.'

'Cowardly man.'

And as Hercules ran off through the trees with Menalippe slung across his unprotected back, he could hear Hippolyta's taunts following him. 'Cowardly man! Cowardly man!'

11

Holding up Heaven

'It's simple,' said Admeta, primping up and down in front of a mirror. 'It's so simple, I don't know why you haven't thought of it before.' The belt of Hippolyta, hitched up in both hands, was much too broad for her hips, and the weight of it pulled her robe out of shape. Its tassels trailed on the floor between her feet, though all the servants in Argos were quick to admire her finery. 'If you can't be rid of him, all you have to do is to set him an impossible task and then execute him for failing.'

'How "impossible"? I keep doing that,' whined Eurystheus.

'Well . . . *impossible*. I mean tell him to fly without wings, or walk on water, or climb up a sunbeam. Tell him to go to the Red Island by way of dry land . . . Look what your precious Hercules has done now, father! This nasty old belt has snagged my favourite dress!'

Eurystheus was peering short-sightedly at the maps on the wall. 'Red Island . . . Red Island,' he mumbled. 'Where is this Red Island, daughter dear?'

Admeta stamped her foot in irritation. 'Oh, *Daddy*! You're so *stupid*. The Red Island doesn't exist. That's the whole point! It's the place in the fairy tales where the giant Geryon and his two-headed dog guard the magic oxen. Everybody knows that story. Everyone knows the Red Island doesn't exist.'

Eurystheus looked crestfallen. It was a long time before the reasoning behind Admeta's plot sank in. 'You mean he *couldn't* get there so he's bound to fail.'

Admeta pulled a face which made her small features still more shrewish. 'Brilliant,' she said.

The king flinched under his daughter's rudeness, but only as the great bison flinches under the peck of birds. He sent for Hercules.

It was perhaps fortunate that Hercules had never heard the fairy tale of Geryon and his oxen. He did not know that the Red Island was the invention of mothers to frighten their naughty children: 'Behave now or Geryon and his two-headed dog will come and carry you away to the Red Island.' He set off willingly enough to fetch back the giant oxen, and he travelled south and he searched.

And he searched and he searched and he searched. And every time he asked for directions, people laughed at him but would not say why. At long last he sat on the southern beach, in the shadow of Mount Abyla, his reins over his shoulder, and he threw irritable stones at the tedious, crawling sea.

'Whaaa?' screamed the seagulls.

'I'm looking for the Red Island and the Giant Geryon!' called Hercules to the seagulls.

'Yeah, yeah,' shrieked the seagulls, darting out to sea along the blood-red line of the setting sun.

He shielded his eyes against the glare and saw that indeed the whole bulk of Africa spread out on the far side of the straits glowed red beneath the setting sun. Hercules was not fond of swimming. He considered the geography for some time—the tall mountain of Abyla behind him and the high profile of Mount Calpe on the far shore. Then, in order to reach the mythical Red Island, he did what men can only do in fairy tales. He leaned his shoulder against Abyla and he pushed. He pushed till the sweat stood in the pores of his skin and bellowed. He pushed till his muscles plaited and replaited. He pushed till the soles of his feet gouged deep gorges in the ground. He pushed till his eyeballs hammered on his lids. He pushed till the rocks of Abyla dented and grooved his flesh and cut through to the bone.

Abyla leaned over. It ducked its granite head which Hercules held down with his feet like the neck of a defeated opponent. Then he reached out with both hands and pulled on the peak of Calpe. He pulled until his shoulderblades stood out like the remnants of wings. He pulled until his spine bowed through the hairs of his back. He pulled until his handprints sank deep in the peak of Calpe. He pulled until the two mountain peaks clashed beneath him and an arch greater than any bridge in the history of Man spanned the Straits of Gibraltar.

No sooner was he across than a man with three bodies stumbled up the slopes of Calpe towards him. Geryon walked like a trio of drunken men leaning against each other for support. His six feet tripped each other up and his six hands waved to steady him. Behind him ran a two-headed dog of awesome size, though its need to smell each bush and tree with both noses made it lag far behind.

'People say I don't exist,' ranted Geryon, clawing his way up the hillside in a hysteria of rage. 'Now they'll see. Now they'll find a mangled body floating in the sea and say—no one could have done that but Gery—oh!' One foot tripped another, a third dislodged the stone four of his hands were holding on to. The boulder overturned. Geryon fell backwards. As he scrabbled and fell, fell and scrabbled, he started a landslip that triggered an avalanche that swallowed up both ogre and ravening dog and stopped short only a few paces from a herd of glossy oxen grazing in the valley below.

Quickly, Hercules herded them together. The join between Calpe and Abyla was already groaning like the ice floes that split in spring. No sooner had he driven the cattle to the mainland, than the peaks sprang apart.

And those who saw it, or heard of it, told a new story to their wayward, sleepy children—'Bed now, or Hercules will come and do to you what he did to Geryon.' They renamed the twin mountains The Pillars of Hercules.

'But he doesn't exist!' said Eurystheus from inside his box.

'No, he doesn't any more,' said Hercules, somewhat confused, 'though I hope you won't believe what people are saying. I never laid a finger on him. He just fell.'

'But he doesn't exist,' said Eurystheus. 'Neither does his dog.'

'I'm sorry about the dog,' said Hercules, and utterly bewildered he left the audience chamber and the king of Argos in his brass hidey-hole muttering, 'Doesn't exist. Doesn't exist. Doesn't exist.'

Outside in the garden, a hundred and thirty-two giant oxen chewed on the flowers.

The obnoxious Princess Admeta was her own undoing. When Eurystheus was at his wits' end wondering what to do with a hundred and thirty-two giant oxen, she gave no thought at all to the problem. She was obsessed with a new idea.

'I know what Hercules can get me! I've been reading about them in religious education,' she said shrilly through a mouthful of shelled nuts. Just as the servants succeeded in mustering the cattle in one place, her piercing voice scattered them again. They startled the Cerynian deer out of the laurel walk and it leapt across a pile of terracotta pots, smashing them.

'What can Hercules bring you? Is it live?' asked the king wearily.

'No.'

'Is it dangerous?'

'No.'

'Is it big?'

'No!'

'Very well, then, my darling dear. You tell him. Only first tell him to come and take these oxen away.'

Admeta did not bother to tell Hercules to help with the cattle. She was in too much of a hurry to have her own way. 'Come and kneel here, slave,' she commanded, perched on the edge of her father's throne and pointing at the floor. 'You're to do everything I tell you from now on. Father says so. I command you to bring me the Apples of the Hesperides!'

'But, mistress! They belong to Zeus, father of all g—'

'Don't argue. I'll have you flogged if you argue.'

' . . . the goddess Hera gave them to Zeus on the day they were married!'

'Servants! Come here this instant and throw this disobedient dog out of the city, and don't let him back in unless he brings what I told him.'

Hercules looked around for the king, but he was out-of-doors, struggling with the oxen. There was nothing to be done—no one he could appeal to for common sense. 'Shouldn't I go and help with the cattle?' said Hercules anxiously.

'You're just trying to put off going. You're frightened of the dragon, aren't you? That's your trouble,' sneered the princess. 'Take your horrible person out of my sight this instant. You make my eyes dirty just looking at you.'

His face, behind his beard, showed nothing, nothing at all. But once outside the palace, Hercules leapt on to his sea-horse with a great savage cry and galloped all the way back to the Pillars of Hercules. He leapt the Straits of Gibraltar into distant Africa. He ploughed on beyond the land of the Amazons to the unmapped undercurve of the world's fat Equator.

There it was so hot that the sea-horse of Poseidon beneath him dissolved into steam and let him fall, on hands and knees, on to a desert plain. He lifted his hands in the air and cried: 'Oh, you gods, what can I do? Must I disobey the master you bound me to? Or must I steal from the gods themselves? Those apples are the property of Zeus the Almighty—his wedding present from Hera his bride!'

From very few points on the Earth's wrinkled landscape would the words of Hercules have failed to reach heaven. But now they came echoing back off the shoulder of a vast mountain. It was late evening. The shape of the mountain was hard to make out against the darkness of the sky. It was simply a shape bare of stars, a shape not unlike a crouching man.

'Quiet down there! A little peace and quiet, if you please. Take my advice and don't appeal against your fate to the gods. Reasonableness and pity are in short supply on the slopes of Olympus. I see the gods every day, squabbling, and gambling with the lives of men. My head is on a level with the highest terraces of Olympus, you see.'

'Who are you?' whispered Hercules as sudden tropical nightfall smothered him like a blanket.

'I am Atlas. Strange that you should bump into me, so to speak.'

'Atlas? The father of the Hesperides? The giant? But I can't see you! Where are you? It's so dark!'

'People mistake me,' said Atlas in a vague, baleful voice. 'They take me for a mountain. Earth and loam and rocks. Can you believe that? Earth and loam and rocks.'

Hercules's mind was whirling. 'Do you visit your daughters often?'

'Don't talk nonsense, boy! How can I go anywhere? I have to stand here and hold up the sky. You think *your* fate is hard? You should try this one day.'

'All right,' said Hercules, his eyes gradually becoming accustomed to the dark. 'I'll stand in for you. You deserve a rest.'

'You?' The ground rocked with laughter, and a star or two fell with green luminosity off the shoulders of the giant Atlas.

'I am Hercules, the son of Zeus.'

Jungle noises, whistles, screeches, and hoots filled up the very long pause. 'Are you? Are you, indeed?'

'Oh, but now I think of it, I can't. I must search out the Gardens of the Hesperides and ask for the golden apples that hang there.'

'Do you know where they are?'

'No,' said Hercules.

'Do you know what the dragon would do to you before you could pick the apples?'

'No, what? I'm not good with dragons. Are you? Do you know the dragon in question?'

'Oh, I knew him as a lizard, boy. He'd do anything for me. Splendid dragon. About this matter of holding up . . .'

'So you could pick the apples of Zeus without any difficulty. Unlike me.'

Again there was a long, cacophanous silence and then, 'See here, Hercules. What say I go and get these apples for you, while you hold up heaven for a while.'

'Done,' said Hercules, quickly sealing the bargain.

Rather than offend the gods in the twelfth and final year of his Labours, Hercules would willingly have lifted the Earth itself in his teeth and juggled with the planets. That was why he had offered to take Atlas's place. But as he crouched in the lee of towering Atlas and let the giant lower the sky's mass on to his shoulders, he did wonder whether the load would crush him to death on the spot.

The first touch of the sky was soft and velvety, though the stars' heat pricked, and meteorite dust blasted his skin like a sandstorm. It seemed bearable at first, but Atlas's hands were still taking the weight. As he let go, it was not like a weight but like a pushing, a pressing, a bearing down—like the force of gravity that pins men to the spinning Earth like a collection of butterflies, but doubled and redoubled and full of burning stars. Frozen comets ricocheted past his head. The muscles of his back plaited and replaited; the soles of his feet sank into the ground; his eyeballs hammered against his lids, and the sweat burst from his eye sockets. The blood roared in his ears; the branching blood vessels of his throat throbbed like serpents, and the vertebrae of his back ground together with the sound of pain. And all the while, the stars stubbed themselves out against his back like so many candles. Inside him, his big heart beat with such an agony of effort that far away on Olympus the gods thought a distant door had been left to bang.

Atlas went to the Gardens of the Hesperides—that realm of paradise beneath the setting sun, where a blood-red tide breaks against salmon pink shores. The air is combed with fingers of rosy cloud, and the green flash of sunset leafs out the trees where hang the apples of Hera. A dragon scaled blue-green coils its sheen around the trunks of milk-white wood, and the sun and the moon hang at either end of heaven for ever and ever and ever.

He had no difficulty in taking the apples given by Hera to Zeus on their wedding day. His daughters and his dragon made no complaint, such was their delight at seeing him free of his burden of sky. His stoop straightened. His muscles eased with creaking noises like the graunching of icebergs, and for the first time in two thousand years, he looked around him at a landscape other than the sear African plain. Atlas stretched, arching his scarred back. A flock of birds flew past his head, wheeling and gliding for no purpose but to celebrate their freedom. The muscle-bound sea strained against its chaining tides. Atlas felt good to be free.

Holding the apples like two golden planets in the palm of one hand, Atlas went back to the central plains of Africa and saw the antelope herds bound tree-high, and the solitary jackals pattering over their limitless territories. He envied their freedom.

Hercules saw him coming, though his face was so clenched with pain that he could barely see or hear or breathe. His legs had buckled, his knees were resting on the sharp rocks and spiky shrub. The sky had sagged just a little, and there and here stars kindled the tallest trees of the highest mountains. Sweat soaked the skin of the Nemean lion and dripped off its snout. Asteroids thudded into his head and chest. Hercules held his life between his grinding teeth and thanked the gods in his heart for the sight of Atlas coming back.

'I've given the matter some thought,' said Atlas, sitting down in front of Hercules and studying his face with a mixture of contempt and pleasure. 'I've lost the taste for holding up the heavens. Since you've made such a fine job of standing in for me, I think I shall let you go on doing it.'

12

Digging up Hell

'I'll deliver these apples to this little king of yours. I'm sure he'll find some way of rewarding me. It's the least I can do for you, after all.'

Hercules's tongue was so dry that it would not stir at first. His throat could only croak, 'Willingly. This is less of a burden than the Labours Eurystheus set me to.'

Atlas was startled. 'You don't mind?'

'Not at all. Pleasure. Easy work. Peaceful,' grunted Hercules in agony. 'One thing. Cloth. Cloth pad . . . across shoulders. Stars. Keep burning. Just lift . . . a moment . . . while I put a pad . . . ' All the major organs of his body seemed about to burst.

Obligingly Atlas folded a cloth pad out of his loin cloth. 'How shall we do this without dropping heaven?'

'You stand . . . beside. Take the weight . . . for a moment. Slip in pad. Roll heaven . . . back on to . . . me.'

So Atlas crawled in under the sagging skies, held a mere fathom off the ground by Hercules's cracking body. He took the weight, and Hercules took the apples out of his hands while he did so . . . then threw himself on his face and rolled out from under. 'I'm sorry, friend. I shall pity you till the day I die, but I am bound in service to King Eurystheus for another two days. I can't idle his time away holding up heaven. Each man to his own task.'

Atlas gave a great roar of outrage and agony, doomed to continue for a thousand years and a thousand more pinned between heaven and Earth. But Hercules had already run so far and so fast, clutching the golden globes to his chest that the giant's cry sounded in his ears like distant thunder rolling among the Atlas mountains.

King Eurystheus felt it at the foot of his bed as he woke— a hard, round shape like a pebble. 'Where is Hercules?' it said. 'Where have you sent him this time?' He pulled down the covers, but could find nothing there. He did not answer the question.

He put his hand into his pocket at breakfast time, and a small, slithering grass snake crept through his fingers. 'Have you failed me, Eurystheus?' it asked. 'Is he suffering?'

He cut open his loaf of bread, and out flew a crow bigger and blacker than a cat, and buffeted against his face. 'His time is almost up. Will you let him escape his doom alive? Will you rob me of my revenge?' croaked the crow and sat on his shoulder and could not be dislodged.

When the servants announced Hercules, the king tried to say he was busy, that he could not see Hercules, that he would see him tomorrow. But the crow sank its talons into his shoulder and whispered in his ear, 'Tomorrow Hercules's sentence is finished. He'll be free. He'll go back to Thebes alive. He'll escape, you fool!'

So Hercules was admitted. 'I have brought what I was told to bring,' he said.

'Good, good. Fine. Just keep them. I don't want them now. I don't have anywhere to put them . . .'

Then Admeta burst into the room. 'Hercules! Have you got them? Where are my apples? Give me my apples *at once*, do you hear?'

When the crow on the king's shoulder saw the golden apples—her own present to the Almighty Zeus on the day of their marriage, her rage almost split her in two. 'How dare you! What manner of man are you, Eurystheus? What manner of brat have you spawned?' She flew in his face and tore out his hair. He ran to his brass box, but it was no protection from the anger of the queen of the gods. She filled it to the brim with scorpions, and chased him round the room with fire. She sent ravens and bats to carry Admeta in their claws to the smallest and loneliest outcrop of rock in all the wide oceans, and muddied the waters all around it so that she might never see her own reflection.

His other daughters asked Eurystheus, as he sat with his threadbare head in his hands, 'What shall Hercules do next? Can he fetch something for us now? Tomorrow he'll be free. Won't you tell him to do anything else before he goes?'

The king smashed all the crockery off the table top, and the shards danced and spun across the floor. 'That name! Always that name! It haunts me! I never want to hear his name again, do you hear me? To hell with Hercules, I say. To hell with him!' Abruptly he lifted his head, and in an ape-like, humourless grin bared his teeth. 'Yes. That's it. That'll make him sorry he stayed alive all these twelve years. Tell the wretch to go to hell—to the Realm of Shadows—and fetch back the dog Cerberus who guards the gates of the City of the Dead. And have him swear to complete the task however long it takes.'

Hercules swore.

He cursed, too, and wept, and struck himself on the forehead with a clenched fist. 'So close to my time! So near to my freedom! If my cousin had been merciful he would have set me to this Labour first and not last. To go to the Underworld so weary and old! Oh, you gods, I would rather have gone a young man, to that place no man ever leaves! Now I shall be weary throughout eternity, and start my stay by antagonizing the king of the Dead and stealing his faithful dog.'

All day as he travelled down to the sea, all night as he sailed a fast, black ship single-handedly through the maze of sea-lanes, he wept aloud and rocked his square body on its haunches, and remembered the events that had set him on the path to the Underworld. And in the morning, when the dawn broke like an egg and filled his boat with yellow sunlight, he found he was not alone.

'Your doom is over, Hercules,' said Pallas Athene, tall goddess of the grey eyes.

'Your twelve years are completed,' said Hermes, messenger of the gods, reclining along a cross-tree of the mast.

'But I've sworn . . . ' began Hercules, unmanned by a sudden stab of hope.

'We know what you have sworn, Hercules. That's why we are here—to accompany you to the Underworld and speak to Pluto on your behalf.'

'Is there a chance, then? That he'll listen? I don't mind saying it: I'm more afraid of angering Pluto than any other god, since I have to spend all eternity in his Realm of Shadows.'

Athene blinked slowly. 'He has his good days . . . '

' . . . and his bad days,' said Hermes, folding his hands behind his head and gazing up at the sky. He kept from rolling off the spar with little flickerings of his winged feet. 'The thing about Pluto is that he's an inveterate gambler. You recollect the business with Orpheus and Eurydice? Pluto told Orpheus, yes, you can have your wife back from the dead if you can climb all the way back to the Land of the Living without looking back at her.'

'What happened?' said Hercules.

'Ah well . . . that was one bet Pluto won. Orpheus looked back.'

'Oh, now you've really cheered him up,' said Athene, jabbing her spear at Hermes in vexation. 'The less we dwell on Orpheus the better, I think.'

The Realm of Shadows has a thousand entrances—some gaping cave-mouths in the seashore, some ragged holes at the end of dark sea-lanes, some bottomless shafts concealed by heather from the unwary traveller, some gouged out by the feet of waterfalls. Hercules and his immortal guides approached by way of a giant wound in the flank of Mount Taenarus in Laconia. The passage was lit by the flickering of white bats which had lived for generations without ever finding their way out to the daylight. The tuneless music of water dripped from the high roof.

They paid the ferryman to row them, all three, across the great river Styx which flows between Life and Death and is neither land nor sea, bone nor blood, but dark cartilage twisting through the body of the Earth.

They disembarked at the cold wharf where all journeys end and none begin. And they reached the doors of Hades. There they could go no further, because a dog with three heads stood rending at the air with ravenous jaws. All the passageways and entrances of the Realm of Shadows met in this one place. Looking in all directions at once, Cerberus guarded the Underworld from all but the Dead.

Even Hermes would not go on. Even Athene came to a halt. When Cerberus saw them, he hurled himself to the bitter end of the three chains that bound his three separate necks. One snapped. One the dog bit through. The third he was grinding between jagged teeth when Pluto himself came patrolling. Such was the size of the god of the Dead that he took Cerberus by the scruff of two necks and held him pinned between his immortal knees. 'Sister! Brother! Why do you bring this mortal living man where none but the dead thrive?'

'To make a wager with you,' said Hermes quickly. 'This is Hercules, Prince of Thebes . . . '

'Ah! So! It is you who is responsible for this great pouring in of monsters and despots. These last twelve years they've trooped down to my dens with your name on their lips. What a slayer of giants you turned out to be! One day, when your time is done and you come this way with funeral pennies on your eyes to pay the ferryman, what earthquakes and upheavals there'll be! Your family, the people you've stolen from, beasts and monsters galore—all with scores to settle . . . ' This prospect of Hercules's fate seemed to put Pluto in an excellent mood. 'So you're the famous Hercules, are you? Small, aren't you?'

'Not too small to carry Cerberus back to the Land of the Living,' said Athene.

Pluto's face stiffened. 'You expect me to give him my dog? You're mad.'

'I don't want to keep him,' said Hercules quickly. 'I only want to borrow him. I can bring him back within the day . . . I bet you I can.'

'You and who else?' Pluto snorted with derision. His eyes gleamed. The temptation of the bet was working in his blood. 'All right, then . . . But you gods keep out of this. If this Hercules sprog can carry off Cerberus without help and without weapons and without harm, and fetch him back again, I'll let him. For the sport of it.'

Athene looked at Hermes uneasily. He shrugged. 'We've done what we can. Hercules must save his own skin now.'

The god of the Underworld loosed the chain on the third neck of the giant dog, and opened his knees just enough to let the beast slip out and lunge at Hercules.

Suddenly, a noise sweeter than the continual dripping of water through stone echoed hauntingly off every facet of the rocky Underworld. The six ears of Cerberus twitched. Its single tail thumped on the floor. Someone was playing a lute.

It was Linus, Hercules's music teacher, his body no more than a ragged shred of air, sitting at the head of a nearby passageway, poring over a lute strung with spectra of light. He had carved it out of the roots of trees grown down as deep as the Underworld itself. Round about him stood all Hercules's little children, no older than on the day he had killed them. None of them looked up: it was as if they were unaware of the intruders into their darkness. When Hercules called out to them, they did not lift their heads, but stared intently at Linus's hands, studying his skill.

The music confused and pleasured Cerberus, the giant hound, but not Hercules. He was overwhelmed by remembered sorrows. He lifted the dog, without caring whether or not it turned on him, and lumbered up the cavernous passageway. Not until the sweet tragedy of the music was fading far behind him did he begin to realize what he had done, and Cerberus to realize what was happening to him. The great hound of the Underworld stirred restlessly and snapped with its three giant heads at the walls of rock speeding by. Hercules filled his lungs and sang at the top of his voice all the lullabies his mother had ever sung, all the loud laments he had heard at funerals, all the shanties he had ever heard sailors sing as they hauled up sails cross-tree-high. Cross-tree-high, the hound of hell howled with all its three heads, then they reached sunlight. The dog's subterranean eyes had strained since puppyhood to see through the gloom of the Underworld. Now it gave a violent shudder and pulled in all its heads.

On the voyage from Laconia to Argos, it hung its three heads over the side of the boat and whined, and its six eyes turned a bilious green. It growled and trembled and had only just recovered its spirits when it reached the palace of Eurystheus.

13

A Wedding Gift

'Here it is, but I have to take it back,' said Hercules, opening the door of the throne room and loosing Cerberus into the presence of King Eurystheus.

When he opened the door again an hour later, the hound of hell lay sprawled on its side like a wrecked whale, its paws resting velvety on the dais. Cerberus filled the room. He lay very, very still. 'What's the matter with him?' said Hercules, panic-stricken. 'Eurystheus, what have you done to Pluto's dog? The gods help us both in the after-life if you've hurt Pluto's dog! Eurystheus?'

But there was no sign of Eurystheus, nor of his brass box, nor of his throne, nor his table set for dinner—nor the lamps nor the litter of furniture, nor the maps on the wall of Cerynia, Thrace, Nemea, and Elis. There was just Cerberus.

As Hercules knelt down beside the hound of hell, thinking to find its fur cold, its breath stopped, it gave a great sigh with two of its heads, whiffled its three noses and scratched itself in its sleep. Picking it up and carefully negotiating the door so as not to wake it, Hercules set off for Laconia once more.

Cerberus seemed strangely heavier on the return trip, and slept all the way. Hercules set him down again in the dank groove the dog had worn, over the years, with his clawing and lunging. He was just re-knotting the chains around the three necks when a young man came running. His feet made no noise of footsteps, because, of course, he had only the gauzy traces of his earthly body.

'Go quickly, Hercules! Go before Pluto knows you're here!'

'But I've brought back his dog—I wagered with Pluto that I could . . . '

'I know all that. Everybody here has heard about it. But don't you know how much Pluto hates to lose a bet? He'll never forgive you for succeeding—never forgive you!' Cerberus whiffled and stretched and barked once or twice in his sleep. 'Quickly! You must go! . . . But, Hercules . . . '

'What?'

'My name's Meleager. I have a sister in the land of the living . . . '

'What about her? Does she need help? I'll help if I can.' Hercules was barely listening: his mind was still running on the injustice of a gambler who refuses to lose a bet.

'Not help exactly, Hercules. She needs a husband. And unless I'm completely wrong in my information, you need a wife . . . No, don't interrupt. There isn't time. Ever since the rumours of your Labours began to blow round hell, I've been turning it over in my mind—you and she should marry. Our father is Aeneus—surely you've heard of him! It's a fine family, ours. And now I'm dead before my time, there's nothing I can do to keep my family name from drooping—yes, sir, drooping from fame to forgottenness . . . I know, I know, you think you'll never marry again because of what happened to your first wife. But just visit her, will you? Please just do me the favour of looking her over. She's followed all your exploits. She's always admired you without even seeing you! Don't say no! Don't say anything! Just go!'

A sudden noise startled Cerberus fully awake. Pluto came lunging down the corridors of the Underworld pointing a finger at Hercules: *'Where's my dog?'*

Cerberus jumped up, one head yelping with delight, the others snarling at Hercules and Meleager. It promptly fell over again with a brass-like clank.

'What have you done to my dog!' Pluto's voice climbed towards hysteria.

'Nothing, I swear . . . ' Hercules began to back away.

'Go,' whispered Meleager. 'You won't win an argument.'

'What have you been feeding him?' Pluto's voice echoed off a thousand rock faces.

'Nothing!' called Hercules as he ran. 'Nothing, I swear!'

Pluto pursued him a few steps, then turned back to attend to his dog. 'I can wait, boy,' he said over his shoulder. 'The faster you run, the sooner you'll be back here with me. Every mortal comes here in the end. I'll wait. I'll make a fitting reception for you when you come back with pennies on your eyes and a shroud in place of that lionskin. I'll teach you for shaming me in front of Athene and Hermes! I'll give you to Cerberus for a bone to chew on. My word on it but I will! *What's he been eating?'*

Hercules burst into the painful sunlight and threw himself down on the grassy slopes of Mount Laconia and tore his hair. Which way to go? To Argos? His twelve years of bondage were over. Why go back? Why go back to Thebes? His doom would still be written on the wall, and there would be no wife or children waiting there to greet him, nothing to do but grow old and await his certain appointment with Pluto. Why wander the world in search of adventure? One too many adventures would inevitably bring his brief, mortal life to an end. Whichever way he looked, Death grinned at him with as many faces as Cerberus and the Hydra put together. Despair griped at him: it was harder to bear than the weight of the stars had been on his back.

Then, at a distance, he heard a terrible scream—a scream that froze his blood and emptied his head of all its questions. He ran towards the sound, and found that not one day, not two days, but three days of running brought him to the source of the scream.

He could not make out the sight at first, for the spot ahead was seething with the jerky fluttering of birds which spiralled into the air as Hercules approached. Beneath their circling, a man lay spread-eagled across a rock on his back, chained hand and foot. The gaping wound in his side should have meant that he was dead. But the heaving arch of his ribcage and the kicking of his legs and above all that terrible repeated scream proved that Prometheus was still tormented with life.

'Who did this to you?' Hercules flailed at the repulsive eagles that hovered insolently beyond reach of his fists. From their beaks dangled red pieces of liver.

'It is my punishment,' gasped Prometheus, slumped in the momentary relief from pain. 'I who stole the secret of fire from the gods must lie here for all eternity and have my liver eaten out by eagles. Oh, gods! Never to die! Never to die! Never to be out of the blazing sun and the flies and the freezing night and the rending of the birds!'

An eagle dived impudently past Hercules's head and snatched a sliver of bloody purple from within Prometheus's side. The scream struck Hercules like a blow and made him stagger with grief. He tore off the

Nemean lionskin and engulfed in its folds all the bloodthirsty birds. He smashed the bundle against the ground and jumped on it and shook out the feathers.

Prometheus laid back his tormented head and laughed. 'More will come. The world has more eagles than you have seconds in your life, friend, but I thank you for pitying me.'

Hercules uttered a subhuman groan and, laying his hands to the chains which bound Prometheus he tore them out of the ground, snapped them off at the wrist, and hurled them so high into the sky that they were lost from sight. 'That for the doom of the gods! If they have no more pity than this, I defy them! I despise them! Their cruelty is worse than Diomedes of Thrace or the king of Elis or the Erymanthean pig! One day I must die and keep my appointed meeting with Pluto. But until I do, I'll find what joy there is in this world and defy all you vicious Immortals!'

Prometheus rolled off the rock and crouched beside it, shielding his wounded body with arms and legs made useless by a thousand years of immobility. 'Tell me your name, boy, that I may shame the gods with it wherever I go. How can you break the unbreakable? How can you end the everlasting? For my chains were unbreakable and my doom was everlasting. Who are you?'

'I am Hercules, son of Zeus—but never till today was I ashamed of my origins.'

All meekness, all penitence, all devout fear left Hercules on that day, and he moved under heaven like a scorpion, full of rage.

He no longer saw good cause to be unhappy, when the Underworld gaped with the promise of everlasting misery. So one lonely night he said to himself, 'Why not? Why not go and see Meleager's sister? Perhaps there's a little shred of happiness for Hercules somewhere on this Earth.' And he got up then and there and travelled to the ancestral lands of Aeneus.

None too soon. For he arrived on the day that Deianeira was to be married to a bull.

It was unfortunate, the matter of the bull. There were so many suitors for the hand of Deianeira—who was extremely beautiful—that it had been decided that they should fight for her. One of the suitors, a river god, had taken the unfair advantage of turning himself into a bull and had carried the day. When Hercules arrived, however, he wrestled the bull to a standstill, tore off one of its horns, and there he was—married to Deianeira. It was done without a thought, and none the worse for that, for who ever chose a wife or a husband by reasoned thinking?

This last-moment alternative to a bull came as a great relief to Deianeira. In fact there was no one on the whole wrinkled face of the Earth whom she would rather have married than Hercules. Hercules was famous. Hercules was the son of a god. To marry Hercules was a greater thing to the daughter of warrior Aeneus than to win the hand of a king. True, Hercules was more of a pagan than she had realized, and would not offer up a sacrifice in celebration of his wedding. But after the wedding, when she was alone, she waded into the brook where Hercules had thrown the broken bull-horn, and filled it with fruit and grain from the wedding feast, and laid it on the altar. 'Goddess of Plenty, I offer you this horn of abundance that my happiness may always overflow as it does today and as this horn overflows with good things.'

There was a clatter of hooves behind her, and she noticed that a centaur stood at the door of the temple watching her. Across its back hung a semi-circular blanket of fluffy white wool embroidered with gold. She smiled, and the centaur bowed from the flanks and slipped away. She did not see him again until later.

It was time for bride and groom to leave the wedding feast and travel to the solitude of old Aeneus's home on the far side of the River Evenus. High in the Olympian mountains, it had been raining, and the river was swollen—swollen so high that the torrent had carried away the only bridge. Deianeira was eager to swim across, but Hercules would not hear of it.

Suddenly the centaur was there again beside them. 'Permit me to carry your wife across,' he said. 'You, Hercules, who was taught by a centaur, know what strength there is in our legs.'

So Deianeira straddled the beautiful blanket, and the centaur lowered himself with great elegance into the rushing water.

'Now come with me, and I'll spill horns of plenty in your lap,' he said to his rider in a low voice full of sudden menace.

'No! Who are you?' said the bride in alarm.

'I am Nessus the centaur. I came too late for the competition, or I would have beaten your other so-called suitors. A woman doesn't need winning—she needs taking, and if she's already taken by another, then she must be stolen! I'll take you to the Hill of the Centaurs and make you brood mare to stallions and fighting men!'

'Hercules! Hercules, help me!' Deianeira hurled herself into the rushing water, but the centaur only scooped her up and rocked her in his two arms. 'Not willing? Then I'll take you there and persuade you after.' He swam with the apparent clumsiness and real efficiency of a horse, and his hooves were already gouging the mud of the far shore. Hercules was only halfway across, his hands full of water, his bow slung useless across his back. He could only watch the centaur speeding away across the flood meadows.

On the far bank he knelt on one knee and took the bow off his back, an arrow from its god-given quiver. He took aim, his hands trembling so that the arrowhead bobbed on and off its target, first on Nessus, then on his wife. Her gauzy bridal clothes billowed and blurred the target. Nessus was getting away—it was loose the arrow or lose his bride. Hercules let the string slip from the crook of his fingers, and had stood up and was running before the arrowhead struck home.

It caught Nessus low down in the back—just above the tussock of hair that is a centaur's mane. His brain called to his legs to carry him onwards, but his legs would no longer answer and buckled and betrayed him. He spilled along the ground, with Deianeira pinned beneath him.

It was an age before Hercules could reach them—a full two or three minutes. The centaur twitched, and foam frothed from the corners of his mouth. 'Forgive me, lady. Love drove me to it. The gods have been just. They guided the arrow. My blessings on your marriage. Don't think unkindly of me, I beg you. Quickly—before he comes. Take a present from me in token of my shame. Take the robe off my back. Take it. It's all I have. Sew it into a robe for Hercules. And if ever . . . ' Approaching death rattled in his throat like the seeds in a poppy head. ' . . . if ever Hercules loses his love for you, give him the robe to wear and it will be rekindled . . . oh yes . . . rekindled . . . ' His hooves scrabbled once through the grass, then he turned his face against the ground and died. He did not have time to mention (if he had meant to mention it) that he was the brother of Chiron whom Hercules had killed.

* * *

Perhaps the threat of losing Deianeira made her precious to Hercules. He did not waste time on wondering whether he had married wisely. He simply loved her. And when no torments came raining down from heaven, he dared to hope that the gods had grown bored with him, or had lost sight of him among the trees and lanes of the mazy world.

They had three children, and if it were not for the dreams at night, Hercules might have been happy everlastingly.

14

Revenge and Forgiveness

He dreamed that he was running through the endless caverns of the Underworld pursued by centaurs, giants, hydras, boars, wives, servants and a multitude of dogs. And at the head of the pack ran Pluto, with Cerberus on a leash, shaking the chains that had bound Prometheus to the rock.

As Hercules ran, he searched—peering into the pitch black recesses, scrabbling through cobwebs, pushing aside boulders—without ever finding what he was looking for. He would wake tearing aside the bedclothes, his eyes straining blindly into the dark, and Deianeira would have to soothe him and reassure him and say, 'Who is it you're looking for in your dream, my dear? Who is it you hope you'll find?'

'I don't know. I don't know!' said Hercules, beating his forehead with his fist. 'When I see them, then I'll know.'

On the black cat-walks of night, Hera walked with her daughter, Hebe. Hercules was the furthest thing from her mind. The birth of a child to her had transformed the queen of the gods. No longer did her mind weave intricate plots of torment for mortal men. The fawning flattery of her serpents could not compare with the open, generous love offered her by her own little girl. What would she not have given to ensure that Hebe was always happy?

Already Hebe was a full-grown woman, for there is little childhood for the Immortals on Olympus. Mother and daughter were companions to each other, and gossiped endlessly about the other gods.

Only one niggling anxiety found room in Hera's breast. Every day, morning and evening, she saw her daughter lying along the parapets of heaven staring down at the Earth below. And Hera did not know—she simply did not know—what animal, what place, what person, what thing her daughter was searching for.

At last Hercules dreamed his dream through to the very end. His legs were failing, his breath was running short, the silent footsteps of the Dead behind were gaining on him, when all of a sudden a voice said, 'Here! Hide here, Hercules!'

The grey, bulging shape of a grotesque cactus grew out of the arid stone floor of the Underworld, with beckoning, spiny limbs. And perched high up amidst the needles sat Iole, the love of his childhood, the crown of her red hair bleached gold for all there was no sun overhead. She reached out her arms as if to help him up into the cactus, and it seemed that the needles were not thorny at all, but soft like the hairs on a peach. He had just taken hold of her hand when a great paw fell on his shoulder and shook him . . .

'Hercules. Hercules, my dear! Wake up. You're dreaming your dream again. Wake up!'

113

'Iole!' Before he was properly awake, Hercules roughly prised his wife's fingers off his shoulder.

'What's Iole?' asked Deianeira.

'A girl . . . someone I knew a long time ago . . . ' He struggled to break free of his heavy sleep. 'Yes! Now I understand what the dream was trying to tell me! There's a vow I never kept. That's what's been preying on my mind. I must go there. I must go now. The dreams will stop if I keep my vow!' His face, even through his beard, displayed a fierce frenzy of feelings, and he got up at once and pulled on the Nemean lionskin, knotting the paws around his waist. 'Kiss the children for me,' he said, and was gone, without shirt, without cloak, without weapon.

Deianeira's reaction was not unreasonable. Without explanation her husband had woken up in the night speaking a girl's name, and had left the house without a backward glance. First she cried, then she was angry, and then she said calmly to herself, 'Let's find out the truth here.' So she sent a letter to Thebes, to Hercules's stepfather, the lonely King Amphitryon. The letter simply said:

'Dear stepfather-in-law, pray enlighten me. Who is the Lady Iole?'

Amphitryon was getting old. But he racked his failing brains and after a time recalled the distant events of Hercules's childhood. He wrote back: *'Dear stepdaughter-in-law, I believe Hercules once felt himself bound to marry the Princess Iole of Oechalia. There are times when I wish he had. Permit me to beg an early visit from you both. Thebes is an empty place these days. Pray tell Hercules I bear no bitterness towards him.'*

Deianeira could not read so far. Her tears obliterated the final words and she screwed the letter into a ball and threw it into the fire. 'So that's your vow, is it, Hercules? To marry Princess Iole. And what about your wife? And what about your children? Oh, Hercules! Is this how the hero of the world behaves now that his Labours are over? No guilt? No conscience? No decency? No love left for me?' Her voice broke and she could not call her servant. She clapped her hands loud and long instead, and when the servant came, she bundled into his arms a rough and ready parcel of cloth. 'Take this robe to Oechalia. You'll find your master there. I hear it is cold there at this time of year. Beg him, for the love . . . no, say, for the duty he bears his wife, to wear this robe. Go! Now! Hurry!' The puzzled servant ran from the room, snagging a trailing corner of the white wool robe against the splintery door. 'Oh, Nessus! If only you were alive today! I could thank you for your present. Oh, I pray its magic is powerful enough to bring him back to me! Is any magic strong enough to mend a love that's broken?'

'No!' cried Hebe, and her hands clawed little pieces of plaster from the parapets of heaven: they fell as unseasonable snow. Quiet and still by nature, the daughter of Hera ran through the long corridors of heaven rending at the thin air as though it were dense undergrowth slowing her down. 'Mother! Mother! Don't let him put on the robe!'

Hera heard her daughter's voice and ran and caught her up in her arms and shook out of her a storm of tears.

'Don't let him put on the robe! Don't let him put on the robe!'

'Who, daughter? What robe? In the name of your father and all the gods, what's the matter?'

Hebe dragged her by the hand to the edge of a terrace and pointed frantically down towards the mosaic patterns of the blue-green earth. 'Hercules! Don't let Hercules put on the robe! Don't you understand? I love him! I love him! I love him!'

The name was like a slap to Hera. Her face emptied of expression. Her grip tightened on her daughter's wrist until the hand turned white and cold. Her lips thinned to a short white slit in her eternally lovely face, and her large, brown eyes narrowed. 'You *love* Hercules of Thebes?'

'Ever since I knew the meaning of the word!' said Hebe. Ignorant of her mother's hatred for Hercules, Hebe went on pleading, 'Don't let him put on the robe! Stop him! Warn him before it's too late!' She felt as if she was shouting at the deaf or shouting at the dead.

At last, after an eternity in the lives of the Immortals, Hera seemed to wake out of a deep sleep. Her mouth relaxed, her cheeks unstiffened, her brown eyes were replenished with affection. 'Tell me about the robe. I know nothing about any robe.'

It was true. She did not. The revenge of Nessus was all of his own devising.

It was cold. Deianeira sat gazing into the fire, murmuring prayers to the goddess of love. It took a long time before the persistent banging of the door in the wind disturbed her. She looked up—and saw that the door was unlatched. A fume of mist seemed to be creeping round it from outdoors. But then she saw that the door itself was smoking, glowing, charring, blackening. She threw a jug of water at it, but to no effect. A few white fibres of the robe were caught in the splinters by the latch and no water, no smothering would extinguish the fire. They had to chop down the door to save the house, and the wood burned to ashes and the latch melted to a shapeless mass.

'No!' screamed Deianeira. 'You gods in heaven, what

have I done? Don't let him put on the robe! Take my life, but don't let him put on the robe.'

'Iole.'

'Hercules.'

She had aged more than in his dream, but not much more. She wore her red hair up, so that he could not see whether the crown was still golden. But her shape was still as musical as a lute, and her eyes were still as green as the unripe pears of cactuses.

'I came here to keep my vow. I vowed to kill your father for cheating me out of marriage to you.'

She looked at him for a long time. She too had wanted that childhood marriage. At last she said, 'My father is already dead, Hercules. And I'm sure the gods would forgive the breaking of such an angry vow.'

Hercules was dejected. He was like a fighting ship suddenly becalmed. 'I no longer care what the gods want or don't want. I just wanted to keep faith with myself. I wanted to keep that vow and kill your father. I hope you understand.'

Iole took hold of his beard in her two hands and shook him gently. 'What kind of way is that to talk? You sound like a heathen. Not care about the gods? Your Labours are over, aren't they?'

'Yes.'

'And they've made you famous throughout the world, haven't they?'

'Yes.'

'And now you have a wife of good family and three lovely children, haven't you?'

'Yes.'

'And you can relax and be still the rest of your life. Would you want things any other way?'

117

'I would rather have married you, Iole, and travelled the world sleeping in cactus bushes and eating worms . . . '

'But I would have made you be a good, devout Greek and make sacrifice to the gods. What's all this about? It's not like you to be so stubborn.'

So Hercules began to explain about Prometheus and the bad temper of Pluto and the fate that awaited him through all eternity. 'Whatever I do—whether I honour the gods or defy them, they'll shovel me into that pit of darkness in the end, with all the people and beasts I've hunted or killed or offended. I'm afraid I can't see the use or the reason any more for saying my prayers—' He broke off when he saw his own house-servant running up the path towards Iole's villa.

Breathlessly the servant knelt down and presented a parcel of cloth to Hercules. 'Your wife begs you to wear this robe to keep you from catching cold.'

'How strange,' said Hercules, somewhat embarrassed in front of Iole. 'She knows I don't feel the cold.' He shook out the robe. 'Kind thought, but I really don't . . . Do you think I should make sacrifice to the gods, Iole?'

'To thank them for giving you such a considerate wife, yes,' said Iole firmly. 'To thank them for an end to your Labours. To ask them for a long, peaceful life and perhaps even their protection when you have at last to go down to the Underworld.'

'I will! I'll go and do it now—if you'll come with me!' The robe dropped to the ground, forgotten. 'Dear, sensible Iole. You always know best. I'm sure you're the wisest person I know. And you don't care whether I'm strong or weak, do you?'

'I just like you for yourself,' said Iole.

'That's why you were there in my dream, rescuing me . . . If only I had married you at the very beginning.'

'Shshsh.' She blushed. 'You can't go and make sacrifice dressed like that. You must wash and change.'

So Hercules laid aside the Nemean lionskin that had always protected his body, and he washed.

'You can wear this robe,' said Iole picking it up. 'It's a fine robe . . . and a token of love from your wife, I'm certain.'

'No!' cried Hebe from the parapets of heaven.

'No!' cried Deianeira as she rode into view of the villa and saw the white robe flash orange in the light of the setting sun as Hercules pulled it on over his head.

'When I make sacrifice, I shall thank the gods chiefly for you, Iole,' said Hercules, easing the shirt over his broad shoulders.

'*No!*' cried Hebe, covering her eyes.

'*No!*' cried Hera, seizing her daughter as she went to leap off the parapets of heaven.

'*No!*' cried Iole, seeing the hairs of Hercules's chest catch light and shrivel.

'NO!' cried Hercules as the robe cleaved to his flesh, every fibre meshing with the hairs of his body before trickling liquid fire through the pores of his skin. The deceitful centaur's revenge was terrible.

Iole ran for water to dowse the fire. She smothered Hercules with a blanket, but the fire would not go out. She burned her hands in beating at the flames, but the fire would not go out.

Though his body was blazing with a red more fierce than the raw sunset, all Hercules's mind could see were dark visions of the Underworld gaping, to swallow him up. An eternity of torment among his victims and enemies, under the peevish eyes of Pluto, under the reproachful eyes of his dead children, under the jaws of Cerberus, under the spite of the gods. The Hydra beckoned him, and Geryon clawed his way out of the ground. And all the while the robe burned without turning to ash and Hercules's body burned through to his soul, and still he did not die.

'Zeus take pity!' cried Iole. 'Let him die! Let him die!'

'Zeus take pity!' cried Deianeira.

'Zeus take pity!' cried Hebe to her father. 'Let him not go forever into the Underworld!'

'Husband take pity,' said the queen of the gods, dropping to her knees alongside her daughter.

But almighty Zeus hesitated, watching his son burn.

'*Zeus take pity!*' cried Hercules, reaching his hands towards heaven.

'It is done,' said Zeus the Almighty in that instant. 'That is all I wanted. Hear this, you gods great and small. My son shall not live out eternity in the Underworld. The mortal in him is purged away, and the hero shall remain, immortal, and live here among us. Wife—let the Earth's beasts and monsters and tyrants look up from every part of the blue-green planet and remember the Labours of Hercules!'

So, as a smithy takes up the white-hot metal in his tongs, Hera snatched up the blazing brand that was Hercules between two beams of the setting sun, and plunged him into the cold of the night sky—the black and sunless void of space spangled by the beastly constellations. The frame of his being was picked out in seven bright stars—shoulders, knees, and head between the centaur-shape of Chiron and the venom-drained Crab of light.

But his soul drifted, like constellar dust, out of the frame of stars and settled on the slopes of Olympus. There little Hebe pasted it together with tears into the husband she longed for, the husband she had longed for, for so very, very long.

Looking at the night sky, it seems that the stars which trace out Hercules are gradually expanding. Over the centuries, the constellation would seem to be failing, falling apart, disbanding as a party disbands when the music comes to an end.

But do not be deceived. The stars seem further apart only because the Earth is swinging in towards the centre of the constellation, pulled by the giant strength of gravity. One day, a million million years from now, the Sun's small family of planets will lose itself among the seven stars, and we shall be cradled in Hercules's arms. All of Earth's little gods, people, beasts, and children will fill that icy emptiness that presently lingers over his heart.